THE ULTIMATE GUIDE TO
STORYTELLING
IN BUSINESS

A PROVEN, SEVEN-STEP APPROACH TO DELIVER
BUSINESS-CRITICAL MESSAGES WITH IMPACT

SAMIR PARIKH

Registered Office(s)
John Wiley & Sons Ltd, The Atrium, Southern Gate, Chichester, West Sussex, PO19 8SQ, UK
John Wiley & Sons, Inc., 111 River Street, Hoboken, NJ 07030, USA

Editorial Office
The Atrium, Southern Gate, Chichester, West Sussex, PO19 8SQ, UK

For details of our global editorial offices, customer services, and more information about Wiley products visit us at www.wiley.com.

Wiley also publishes its books in a variety of electronic formats and by print-on-demand. Some content that appears in standard print versions of this book may not be available in other formats.

Library of Congress Cataloging-in-Publication Data

Names: Parikh, Samir, 1970- author.
Title: The ultimate guide to storytelling in business : a proven, seven-step approach to deliver business-critical messages with impact / Samir Parikh.
Description: Hoboken, NJ : John Wiley & Sons, Inc., 2024. | Includes index.
Identifiers: LCCN 2023049007 (print) | LCCN 2023049008 (ebook) | ISBN 9781394234578 (cloth) | ISBN 9781394234592 (adobe pdf) | ISBN 9781394234585 (epub)
Subjects: LCSH: Business communication. | Communication in management. | Storytelling. | Marketing.
Classification: LCC HF5718 .P347 2024 (print) | LCC HF5718 (ebook) | DDC 658.4/5—dc23/eng/20231019
LC record available at https://lccn.loc.gov/2023049007
LC ebook record available at https://lccn.loc.gov/2023049008

Cover Design: Wiley
Cover Image: © hasan kurt/Shutterstock
Author Photo: Courtesy of Samir Parikh
SKY10063841_010524

CONTENTS

ACKNOWLEDGEMENTS

Another great collaboration with my partner-in-crime, Peter Stinner, who has read every word that I have written and shared many interesting insights that helped to shape this work. He has helped many industry professionals to advance their storytelling journeys as an authority on this topic.

Also to my extended review team: Lina Andersson and Shireen Sindi, both senior practitioners who validated the concepts presented within their own industries of expertise. Thank you both for your dedication, contributions, and curiosity.

ABOUT THE AUTHOR

Samir Parikh is a British-born management consultant with over 25 years of industry experience. He began his career in the UK, consulting in the aerospace industry, and then later joined a large international consulting firm where he participated in pan-European projects in the information technology, financial services, and telecommunications industries.

In early 2000, Samir founded SPConsulting, a global management consulting firm based in Stockholm, Sweden. The firm works closely with companies that deliver solutions and professional services in their own areas of specialization and in highly competitive environments. With many of its clients being multinational corporations, SPConsulting has conducted assignments in more than 55 countries.

Storytelling has played an instrumental role in these engagements, crafting impactful messages for both internal and external audiences, to expedite decision making, secure commitment, and exploit new business opportunities. The proven methodology described in this book has been used to create these outcomes and also forms the basis for training workshops delivered to ambitious corporations that aim to make the science of storytelling an essential part of their culture.

INTRODUCTION

How often have you had to deliver a pitch, convey a message or empower an audience with only one chance to get it right? Perhaps a job interview, an important sales presentation, or the announcement of major changes within your organization? Have you ever had a powerful idea that was never adopted because your peers didn't recognize its value?

Storytelling is mission-critical to the advancement of our careers and our businesses.

Storytelling is a powerful, analytical approach to frame and deliver a message. Whether delivered verbally in a meeting, documented in a report, or built into a presentation, it provides a robust approach that's critical in situations where the stakes are high. It enables you to convey a complex idea quickly, win the acceptance of others, speed up decision-making and demonstrate your contributions as a thought leader.

Storytelling is as suited to external discussions with clients as to internal communication. It's as essential to leaders in mobilizing their organizations as to young professionals aiming to accelerate their careers. In the world of storytelling, less is more. It's the cure for lengthy presentations that take days to prepare and hours to listen to and increases impact by getting to the point quickly. It will enable you to distill a complex, 30-page report into a 1-minute verbal account or a 5-paragraph executive summary with minimal effort.

The storytelling methodology described in this book is well proven. It has been developed based on years of experience building business-critical stories around multi-million-dollar sales opportunities, strategic change initiatives, the introduction of new business models, and the launches of ground-breaking technical ideas.

As you might imagine, delivering these stories hasn't always been a walk in the park. Some audiences have been receptive, others have been skeptical. We've had to deal with resistance, political agendas, and even warfare in the boardroom. The ability to handle these obstacles is an essential part of storytelling and can be the key to reaching a successful outcome.

This book is organized as a story in itself. It will take you on a practical journey illustrated by real-world examples and case studies. Be sure to apply the new ideas that you learn quickly. What you apply successfully will become a habit. Mistakes that you make along the way will become insightful lessons. Both will become valuable assets for the future.

Quoted by one of our clients:

> *"Some of our experts don't feel comfortable when asked to tell stories. It's a skill that they feel that some people are just born with. This methodology provides a more scientific approach that enables anyone to excel in storytelling!"*

Storytelling requires a different approach in business

Storytelling is a broad term. It can refer to everything from the bedtime story that sends your child to sleep to the presentation of a pivotal initiative to senior executives. Many texts on the topic lean heavily toward the needs of fiction writers. While many of the principles are similar, storytelling in the business context requires some additional considerations. Let's illustrate this with a simple definition:

> **Storytelling is an approach to both build and deliver robust and accurately customized messages that inspire audience acceptance and action in business-critical situations.**

Storytelling is indeed an **approach** with a supporting mechanism behind it. Its structured, reliable, and repeatable nature enables us to build effective stories again and again.

An effective story takes the audience on a journey and needs to be **customized** to their needs and interests.

Otherwise, why should people listen? Customized messages resonate with an audience, capturing their attention and inspiring them. Generic messages go over their heads, their minds quickly drifting elsewhere.

The stories that we build in business are designed to inspire **action**. Securing actionable outcomes is perhaps one of the most challenging tasks, but an essential skill. If you deliver a presentation to your peers or clients and nothing happens afterwards, you probably wasted your time.

And **business-critical** refers to situations where the price of failure is extremely high. An unsuccessful sales presentation comes with a cost. A poorly explained company re-organization may result in employees seeking jobs elsewhere. And a senior leader presenting to the media faces the same challenge. If she doesn't make a good speech, she may damage her personal brand and that of her organization.

A methodology based on seven logical steps

Our storytelling methodology is built on seven logical steps, each of which has an important role to play. Seven steps might sound like a lot of work, but due to its very logical nature the approach quickly becomes intuitive.

Every time that you build a story, imagine you are solving a unique puzzle. The methodology is your solution guide (Figure 0.1). Let's briefly introduce each of the seven steps:

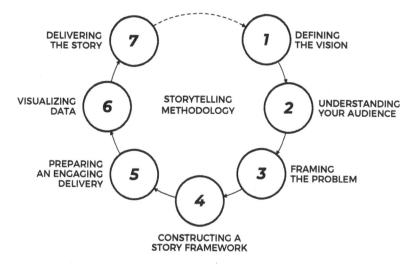

Figure 0.1: Storytelling methodology

1. **Defining the vision:** A good story needs a clear vision. Ask yourself the question: 'What outcome should result from the delivery of this story?' Start with the goal in mind. This doesn't have to be a complex task, but the scope and ambition level of the story must be clear.

   We'll show you how to define the vision for a story and introduce some common pitfalls to be avoided. Defining the vision correctly is important, as everything that you build into the story will point back to it.

2. **Understanding your audience:** A successful story needs to appeal to the interests, priorities, and potential concerns of the receiving audience. A good understanding of your audience is therefore essential.

   We'll introduce a simple method for profiling an audience before you build a story and demonstrate how the information collected can be woven into its framework. This ensures that the story will reflect the reality of the audience and that it will resonate with them.

3. **Framing the problem:** Many of the issues that we build stories to address are vaguely specified from the outset. That makes it difficult to build a story that's guaranteed to hit the target with high certainty. We need to frame the problem before we can build a story to solve the problem!

We will introduce a framing technique that will have an instrumental impact on the content of your story and, in turn, your ability to achieve your vision.

4. **Constructing a story framework:** Constructing a story framework is the heart of the storytelling process. It's an important analytical exercise requiring a structured approach. Successful stories in business rely on a collection of logical arguments, the building blocks that we use to build our stories.

We'll show you two different ways to build an argument and illustrate how these can be combined into the framework of the story. The result will be a one-page story blueprint that can be translated into any format needed: a document, a presentation, even a verbal dialogue.

5. **Preparing an engaging delivery:** With a logical framework in place, we are now ready to elaborate the story and prepare the detailed content. The powerful skill of narrating your key messages and managing the dialogue with your audience should not be underestimated and will require some preparation.

We will introduce a set of powerful tools, from the use of linguistic structures to the underlying science of neurochemicals and emotional triggers. We will illustrate the benefits of including characters in a story, the use of descriptive detail, and the importance of crafting an audience interaction approach.

6. **Visualizing data:** Data may play an important part in a story, however, a single data set can be represented in several different ways, each communicating a different message.

   From a psychology perspective, we will introduce the cornerstones of the visualization system that governs the way that we interpret data, together with some simple, but powerful, practices that can be used to elevate the role of data in a story.

7. **Delivering the story:** The successful delivery of a story depends both on its construction but also the way in which it is delivered. Your ability to lead your audience and maintain their interest will play a fundamental role.

   As a presenter, the use of vocal modulation techniques and your ability to create presence, whether on-stage or on-camera, will be essential to audience engagement. And if you are dealing with a senior or critical audience, the smooth handling of questions will be essential to gaining their approval.

   We will introduce the skills required to handle difficult situations and the unexpected. You might be well prepared, but you never know what's going to be on your audience's mind. Priorities may have shifted at the last minute, some participants may be resistant to new ideas, or bring political agendas to the table. It's your ability to deal with these obstacles that will lead to a successful outcome.

These seven steps describe the journey that we take you on as we navigate through this book. Each chapter, corresponding to a step in the methodology, will provide clear guidelines backed by industry examples. Collectively they will equip you with the toolkit needed to excel in storytelling.

Good luck on your storytelling journey!

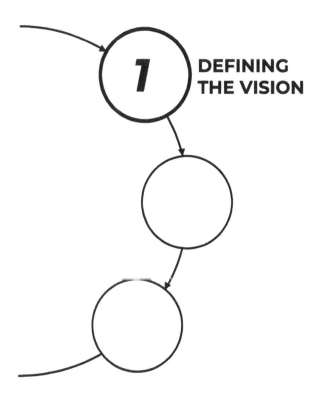

1 DEFINING THE VISION

To take someone on a journey,
you need to know where you're going

CHAPTER ONE

DEFINING THE VISION

A story in business needs a clear vision: a purpose. Everything that you build into the story will point back to that vision. This is where many stories go wrong. A clear vision may either be missing or poorly defined.

It's essential that the vision is outcome-oriented. If the vision is achieved, then you have succeeded. To define it, simply ask yourself the question:

What outcome should result from the delivery of this story?

Defining the vision doesn't have to be a complex task but there are some pitfalls to avoid that would otherwise compromise the effectiveness of the story.

A multinational bank in Europe was about to embark on a major technology project to implement a suite of business support systems required to enhance their internet banking service.

The consulting team supporting this project wanted to advocate the use of a particular methodology (for project planning and control), feeling that their client's routine project management approach was unlikely to be adequate for such a complex engagement.

Alice, the responsible consulting manager, tasked a member of her team, Dan, to build a story around their proposed approach and to build an accompanying presentation.

"Make sure that your material is good", she said. *"In two weeks we need you to fly to Germany and present this story to the client's executives. It's important that we get them on-board."*

Dan got to work enthusiastically. With a strong background in project management, he was well suited to the task. Two days later Alice passed by his desk to check on the progress.

"What is the vision for the story that you are working on?," she asked.

"To inform our client about the strengths of our project planning and control methodology in technology projects," Dan replied.

Now a question to the reader: Is this a good vision for the story? Probably not.

A story's vision should be outcome-oriented, not action-oriented.

To "inform" is an action, not an outcome. In storytelling we don't want to talk for the sake of talking. We need a much higher-arching ambition when we build a story.

Alice explained this to Dan and together they reformulated the vision for their story:

> *To **gain our client's confidence** in the strengths of our planning and control methodology and to ensure that **any associated concerns are understood and addressed**.*

Gaining their client's *confidence* and ensuring that any associated *concerns were understood and addressed* were the two outcomes that they needed to get the green light to move forward.

In this case, the latter part of the vision was particularly important. Their client was often quite conservative. They tended to come to meetings, nod in agreement for an hour and then nothing would happen for 4 weeks. It would be essential for Dan to understand their concerns during the session and find ways to address them before real commitment could be secured.

Dan returned to the development of his story. Inspired by the new vision he shaped the story and its content in quite a different way than he had initially intended.

Two weeks later the presentation was well received by the client executives who subsequently agreed to adopt the proposed methodology.

Six things to consider when defining a vision for your story

When building a story always start by defining a clear vision:

1. **Think about outcomes, not actions.** What outcomes should result from your efforts to build and deliver this story? Make sure that the vision that you define is the one that you really want to achieve. Avoid Dan's mistake!

2. **Make it a formal process. Write it down.** Even for a complex story the vision statement should be one or two sentences at most. Be specific through the prudent use of vocabulary. Everything that you build into your story will point back to this vision.

3. **Remember that the vision is for you.** It's about *your* agenda and the outcome that *you* want to achieve. It's not something that you usually share with your

audience or include in the content of your story. In our example, Dan's vision was not the headline of his story, but the story's flow and content were designed to achieve it.

4. **Ensure that the vision is in-context and refers back to the receiving audience**. The receiving audience should be mentioned in the vision statement, "our client," in the example above. It's important that you define your ambitions relative to your audience.

5. **Make sure that the ambition-level of your vision is realistic.** The vision refers to the outcome to be secured immediately upon completion of the delivery of your story, not the completion of a lengthy project or engagement.

   A vision to "persuade a client to buy a complex solution," after the delivery of a story in an initial one-hour meeting is probably over-ambitious, whereas the vision to "capture a client's interest in the solution and to identify questions that need to be answered moving forward" would be more realistic.

6. **When co-developing a story, align on the vision first**. It's not uncommon for a team to be working together on a story, each member responsible for developing a different part. Start by agreeing on the vision and get everyone on the same page. As a result, your team members will be pulling in the same direction, you'll save time and create a more cohesive result.

Some examples of vision statements

- For a team working in human resources, presenting a diversity strategy to their executive team:

  To gain management approval to move forward with our strategy and to agree on any adjustments that are needed.

- For a sales team, presenting an offering to a client:

  To gain agreement from our client that our offering is superior to that of the incumbent vendor.

- For engineers in research & development, pitching a new idea to marketing and sales:

  To gain alignment with marketing and sales on the best go-to-market strategy, sales approach, and timing for this new offering.

- And for a manager presenting a change initiative to her team:

  To empower our people regarding their achievements, to ensure that they understand why change is needed, and to highlight the opportunities this brings for everyone, addressing any associated concerns.

Chapter summary

- A story in business needs a clear vision: a purpose. Everything that you build into the story will point back to that vision.

- The vision should be outcome-oriented, not action-oriented.

- Make the definition of the vision a formal process. Write it down in one or two sentences.

- Make sure that the ambition-level of the vision is realistic. Can it be achieved upon completion of the delivery of your story?

Next steps

Select a story that you plan to deliver in the near future. Use it as a personal case study as you navigate through this book.

Begin by defining your vision using the guidelines presented in this chapter and note it down. If the vision is achieved when you deliver your story, will you have succeeded?

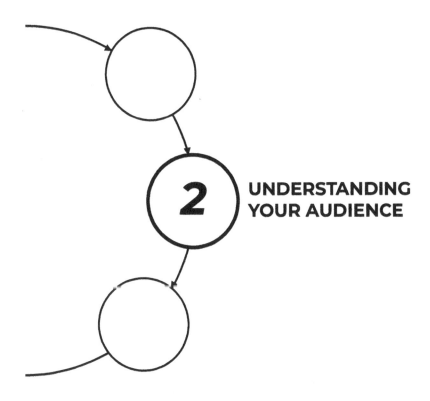

2 UNDERSTANDING YOUR AUDIENCE

When building a story, see the world through the eyes of your audience

CHAPTER TWO

UNDERSTANDING YOUR AUDIENCE

Storytelling is all about your audience. You bring your audience on board by making the story about them and by connecting it to their reality. It's surprising how many stories fail to embrace this, revolving around the ideas and proclamations of the presenter.

Achieving some degree of intimacy with your audience is essential to capturing their attention. Do you know who they are? What's important to them? Their environment? It's also fundamental to your credibility. A seasoned audience will quickly spot whether you've done your homework. Are you presenting generic material or tailoring your message to them?

Chloe, a design architect in North America, had been asked to build a presentation to pitch a new portfolio of services to a potential client in the luxury retail industry.

She spent several hours designing a presentation packed with facts and features to explain the portfolio's strengths. She called a meeting with her manager, Adam, to review the work before meeting with the client later that week.

Adam reviewed the presentation. Chloe had created a good story, elaborated in a set of well-designed presentation slides. The problem was that the presentation was simply a sales push, boasting the attributes of their services.

"Good work, but how do you think that the client will react when you present this?," he asked. *"They probably see presentations like this all the time from other design agencies that are trying to win business. Let's make this story about them, not about us."*

Leveraging their knowledge of the client, they re-engineered the story.

- They started off talking about the client's (published) go-to-market strategy and business aspirations.
- They referred to known challenges that the client was facing as well as issues that they might be experiencing with their current service providers.
- Finally, the last part of the story explained how their company's services could address these needs quickly and accurately.

It was a different story, focused on the interests of the audience rather than the intentions of the presenter.

Three days later when the story was presented, the client responded with great enthusiasm. This was far from a standard pitch, rather a story that had been created for *them*. The discussions that followed resulted in a significant win for Chloe and her organization.

Connecting a story to the interests of an audience clearly requires a good understanding of that audience. This enables you to customize your story, incorporate audience-specific information to make sure that it will resonate. The more you know about your audience, the better, but in a world where time is a scarce resource, the opportunity to gather this information may be limited.

This chapter introduces a simple, three-step approach to accelerate the process. If you only have one hour available to profile an audience, it will show you what to look for. With more time available, it will show you where to dig deeper. And a template will be introduced that can be used to consolidate the information gathered. At the end of the chapter, a case study will illustrate how the approach works in practice.

The three preparation activities required to profile an audience

There are three activities to consider when profiling an audience. We'll start with a scenario where the story is intended for an external audience such as a client or partner, but the approach can be easily adapted for internal audiences by modifying some of the preparation elements.

1. **Basic preparation:** Considers the "must know" information about an audience before you build a story. Basic preparation can generally be completed within one hour as the information is usually easily accessible. If you are short of time, this is the minimum amount of effort to invest.

2. **Detailed preparation:** A more in-depth exercise resulting in a more comprehensive audience understanding. This can be an open-ended exercise but typically requires between half a day and a day to complete.

3. **Stakeholder profiling:** Establishes who your key stakeholders are, their backgrounds, their probable interests, and potential concerns. This is not usually time-consuming and provides a powerful input to the tailoring of your story.

Basic preparation addresses the "must-knows"

Basic preparation captures a fundamental understanding of the organization that you are addressing. It aims to collect the minimum amount of information required for your audience to recognize themselves in the story and for it to resonate.

The list of elements below is not exhaustive and may need to be adapted according to industry specifics but is likely to include:

Industry	Industries that the target organization is addressing (e.g., consumer electronics, healthcare, insurance).
Geography	Geographical scope, office locations. Overseas holdings and ownership in other businesses.
Headquarters	Headquarters location.
Financials	Revenue and profit reported for the last financial year, if published.
Key executives	The names of the top executives and other key stakeholders.
Business units	Business units and their functions, if applicable.
Market position, market share	Competitive position, rank in the industry, market share.
Products and services	The products or services that the target organization is providing and the way in which the offering is structured and priced.
Customers, target segments	Who are the target organization's customers and which segments are they targeting?
Notable customer wins	Notable customer wins and success stories as proof points of the value that the organization can deliver.
Main competitors	Competitors within each product or service segment.
Recent news or promotions	May relate to a wide variety of topics such as campaigns, international expansion, partnerships, acquisitions, or the divesting of non-profitable entities.

Existing relationships	If you have worked with this organization before, leverage your internal intelligence. What engagements have you conducted and what were the outcomes?
Known issues/needs	Consider known issues, sensitivities, business priorities, internal politics, and decision-making culture.

Adapting basic preparation to an internal audience

Basic preparation can easily be adapted to the needs of an internal audience. Consider a training manager asked to build a learning strategy for a manufacturing unit within her organization and to present this as a story.

The preparation elements considered would most likely include the number of employees within the unit, manufacturing locations, annual sales and profit, key internal stakeholders, market position, main competitors in their target segment, product and service offerings, customer wins, metrics used to measure performance, and any known successes or challenges based on internal press releases.

Detailed preparation provides a more in-depth understanding

Detailed preparation brings your audience understanding to the next level. The following elements provide a good starting point and can once again be adapted to the needs of an internal audience:

Strategy, vision, and objectives	The target organization's stated business vision and strategic objectives.
History and key milestones	Key milestones in the company history. These often impact culture and decision-making power, particularly if mergers or acquisitions have taken place.
Notable industry trends	What are the media and industry analysts saying about the future?
Product and service innovation	Published research and development initiatives. Recent market launches and their outcomes.
Sales channels	How does the organization sell its products and services?
Marketing and positioning strategies	How does the business present itself to the market and which values are projected to end-customers?
Operational strategies	May include operational models such as remote service centers and offshoring.
Detailed financials	Such as the breakdown of operating expenses and the contribution of each business unit.

Stakeholder profiling homes in on the interests of individuals

Profile key stakeholders within your audience on an individual level.

In storytelling, we define a key stakeholder as anyone who can either positively or negatively impact the successful achievement of the story's vision.

These usually include decision makers, influencers, and other key people whose support you will need. Consider the following questions:

- **What are their backgrounds?**

  Learn about your key stakeholders. Tools such as LinkedIn can provide valuable insights.

- **What are their probable interests?**

  Think about the roles that they perform, the contributions that they are expected to deliver, and, as a result, their probable interests.

- **What are their potential concerns?**

  What kind of concerns is your topic likely to raise with different stakeholders? For example, recommendations that may be seen as unwelcome, a need to depart from the status quo, and political or perception-related objections.

Leverage both internal and external resources when collecting information

A wide range of information resources can be used when learning about your audience. Some of the most common are:

- **The target organization's website:** Usually a good resource for information such as corporate vision, strategic objectives, corporate values, product and service offering, organization, and geography.

- **Press releases:** Provide a wide variety of information such as recent events, new initiatives, partnerships, acquisitions, and organizational changes.

- **Annual reports:** Provide financial information (income statement, balance sheet, cash flow statement) as well as an introductory account of general performance, strategy execution, diversity and sustainability policies.

- **Analyst reports and industry articles:** Can be very useful in understanding industry trends, market expectations, competitive threats, and potential opportunities.

- **Internet searches:** Can provide a multitude of valuable information regarding people, business transactions, and references. Make sure that any information used is published by a reliable source.

- **Contacts and colleagues:** People within your organization or network who have worked with the target organization or any of the key stakeholders before.

Consolidate the information gathered into a template or repository

Consolidating audience-related information into a template or repository provides an at-a-glance summary and helps you to draw useful conclusions from information that you have collected. Larger organizations use customer relationship management (CRM) systems and data-repositories to store this type of information about their clients.

Case study: SmartStream

This case study, based on a real industry situation, will be used for demonstration purposes and will evolve throughout Chapters 2, 3, 4, and 7.

Jensen Consulting has been engaged by SmartStream, a provider of media streaming services in Northern and Eastern Europe. They have been asked to analyze an important technology issue and present recommendations on the best way forward. They plan to use the storytelling methodology described in this book to structure their approach to this assignment.

SmartStream, offering a wide range of video and audio content, holds a leading position, however, competitors are quickly gaining ground in some of their markets by providing customers with greater flexibility and a richer offering of services.

A particular bottleneck for SmartStream relates to the way in which they bill their customers. Their current billing system lacks flexibility, the ability to accommodate different billing formats, and is unable to support some of the new services that they plan to launch to remain competitive.

Significant investments will be required to overcome these challenges affecting people, processes, and their technology systems. SmartStream suspects they will need to replace their current billing system, a complex project that would take many

> months. They have given Jensen four weeks to analyze the issue and deliver their recommendations in a report. Jensen is also expected to present their findings in a one-hour presentation to SmartStream's executive team.

Using the steps described in this chapter, Jensen has assimilated an understanding of their new client and the probable expectations of the key stakeholders that they will be dealing with. The output is documented in the template below.

Basic preparation

The following information has been collected.

Table 2.1: SmartStream: Basic preparation

Topic	SmartStream
Industry	Provider of media streaming services.
Geography	Europe, five countries (see list below).
Headquarters	Copenhagen, Denmark.
Financials	2022 revenue: 1.1b Euro.
	Operating profit: 227M Euro.
Key executives	Kristian Sorensen (CEO).
	Christina Lassen (CMO).
	Nils Mortensson (CTO).
Business units	Nordic (Denmark, Norway, Sweden).
	Eastern Europe (Croatia, Estonia).
Market share	15% Croatia, 34% Denmark, 28% Estonia, 19% Norway, 25% Sweden.

Topic	SmartStream
Products and services by revenue	Video (films and series) 54%, music 22%, sporting events 15%, podcasts 9%.
Customers and target segments	3.15M subscribers across five countries. Focus on private consumers and small businesses.
Notable customer wins	Rapid growth in Sweden as a new market for the last 2 years.
Main competitors	Other streaming, cable TV and telecommunications providers in each selective market.
Recent news or promotions	"Cheap" campaign in Sweden.
Previous projects	None – first engagement with Jensen.
Known issues/ needs	Actively seeking to create a common technology footprint with the same billing system used in all group countries. Strong focus on cost (OPEX) reduction.

Detailed preparation

The following information has been collected.

Table 2.2: SmartStream: Detailed preparation

Topic	Definition
Strategy, vision, and objectives	To become a customer-centric company providing best-in-class customer service, flexibility, and a rich content offering at a competitive price point. A cornerstone of their strategy is the ability to bring new content and services to market faster than competitors. They aim to enrich their offering through partnerships with other content providers and provide bundled offerings.

(Continued)

Table 2.2: (*Continued*)

Topic	Definition
History and key milestones	Founded in 1996 in Copenhagen, Denmark. Has made acquisitions of several smaller companies to expand their geographical footprint.
Notable industry trends	All of SmartStream's markets are extremely competitive.
Product and service innovation	SmartStream offers different products and services in their different markets. They aim to increase their penetration in the small business segment, but will require more flexible payment and discounting options to achieve this.
Sales channels	Does not have their own branded stores. Focused on web sales, tele-sales, and channel sales.
Marketing and positioning strategies	SmartStream maintains that their success is based upon good quality services and the best price at all times.
Operational strategies	SmartStream constantly seeks selective growth opportunities that meet strict financial targets and fit their corporate culture.
Financials (in Euro)	Revenue: 2022: 1.1b 2021: 944M 2020: 877M Profit: 2022: 170M 2021: 142M 2020: 130M Comments: 2022 revenue increased by 15% year on year with an increase in profit of 20%.

Stakeholder profiling

The following information has been collected.

Table 2.3: SmartStream: Stakeholder profiling

Name	Kristian Sorensen, CEO
Background	Various positions at A.P. Moller-Maersk A/S business conglomerate for 15 years, foremost in transport and logistics. Held a CEO position at subsidiary Maersk Tankers for 4 years before moving to Danske Bank where he joined as the COO. After 7 years Kristian moved on to SmartStream as CEO.
Probable interests	A strong believer that a balance of customer centricity coupled with operational efficiencies will be the keys to SmartStream's success. Keen to improve SmartStream's market position and profitability within its current operations.
Potential concerns	Profitable growth. Balancing investment with the achievement of short- to medium-term returns.

Name	Christina Lassen, CMO
Background	Started at Spotify in Sweden as an intern and worked in different parts of the organization during a rotation program. Was a key player in the development of marketing strategies that became a fundamental part of Spotify's growth in Asia. Based in Shanghai for 5 years where she held a CMO position. Before moving to SmartStream 2 years ago she worked as CMO for Lego Interactive and later for Lego North America.
Probable interests	Christina has been something of a champion since joining SmartStream in seeking to differentiate their portfolio from that of competitors. A lot of effort has been placed on segmentation and targeted marketing strategies.

(Continued)

Table 2.3: (*Continued*)

Name	Christina Lassen, CMO
Potential concerns	Her key concern is time to market and the ability to launch new offerings and tariffs quickly, as well as the capability to offer customized tariffs to meet the needs of the enterprise segment. This is a recognized weakness for SmartStream compared to competitors.

Name	Nils Mortensson, CTO
Background	Graduated from Denmark's leading technology university. Spent the first 10 years of his career at the engineering organization of TeleDanmark. Recruited to SmartStream 5 years ago.
Probable interests	Believes that simplicity will be essential to scalability and operational excellence. High expectations regarding system functionalities that will support them into the future.
Potential concerns	Believes that SmartStream engineering and operations teams are often slow to adopt new ways of working. This has slowed the introduction of new support capabilities in their systems (e.g. billing, customer relationship management) that are needed for the launch of new services.

Putting your audience understanding to work

The chapters that follow will demonstrate the important role that your audience understanding will play in the construction and delivery of the story.

1. A better knowledge of your audience puts you in a better position to engage accurately and with high credibility.

2. It ensures that the story will be relevant to the audience. By incorporating some of this information and by making the story about *them*, it is more likely to resonate.

3. It will enable you to anticipate likely questions and to address concerns when the story is delivered.

Experience from the field

Industry practitioners who have applied the ideas in this chapter shared the following reflections:

"I deliver a lot of presentations to our different (internal) business units. Although it would be hard for me to become an expert in each business area, performing this preparation has made it easier for me to make proactive suggestions that are seen as relevant."

—Procurement Director, accounting and audit, Canada

"Our salespeople tend to go to clients and focus on presenting our solutions. The presentations are mostly about us and what we can do, and not about the clients and their needs. Building this angle into our stories has increased our perceived value as a partner."

—Sales Director, financial services, United Kingdom

"We have worked with some of our clients for many years. We think that we know them, but do we really know them enough? In particular, understanding the client segments that they are serving. Audience understanding is an asset and can always be improved."

—*Outsourcing Manager, real estate services, USA*

"We already profile our clients, but some of the most valuable insights are locked in the heads of a few senior people. This approach demonstrates the need to share the information across our client-facing teams and to make sure that they use it."

—*Account Manager, engineering and automation, Finland*

Chapter summary

- For a story to resonate with an audience, it needs to reflect their reality. Can they recognize themselves in the story?

- Audience preparation allows us to profile an audience and include information that is specific to them within the framework of the story.

  - Basic preparation addresses the "must knows" about an audience before building a story.

  - Detailed preparation is a more in-depth exercise, performed when building an important story and when more time is available.

  - Stakeholder profiling considers the backgrounds, probable interests, and potential concerns of those who could positively or negatively impact the successful achievement of the story's vision.

Next steps

Think about the personal case study that you have selected. Develop your audience understanding by performing:

- Basic preparation
- Detailed preparation
- Stakeholder profiling.

Consolidate your findings into a template as illustrated in this chapter.

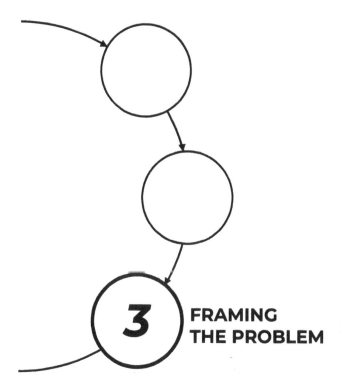

3 FRAMING THE PROBLEM

*A poorly focused approach
is unlikely to hit the target*

CHAPTER THREE

FRAMING THE PROBLEM

Many of the problems that we are required to build stories to address are vaguely specified from the outset. That makes it difficult to build a story that's guaranteed to hit the target with high certainty. Do we really know enough about the problem to build a story that will address the real business needs?

A company asking five different marketing agencies for recommendations on "how to improve its marketing impact" would be presenting a question that is rather open-ended. A likely result would be five different stories, each exploring similar yet different angles. And there's no guarantee that any of them would home in on the company's most critical needs.

The same challenge could apply if you are building a story for an internal audience within your organization. You might be asked by your director to prepare a presentation on "future innovations in your department." You put in your best effort, but having completed the task, you receive the feedback, "This is good, but it's not exactly what I had in mind. . ."

An impactful story combines the expertise of the authors with a clear understanding of the needs of the receiving audience, relative to the issue at hand.

People build stories based on their research and what they know but fail to embrace the importance of what they don't know, relative to the expectations of the audience. Experience has shown that this is where many stories miss the mark.

Framing is the process of creating clarity around what should be in focus and what is irrelevant. Leveraging a process known as *co-creation*, it's an exercise that will help you align with the needs of your stakeholders and define a clear content strategy for your story. In some clear-cut cases you might have this pinned down already, but in others it can be an exercise of instrumental value.

Cheryl, a senior analyst in the aviation industry, has been approached by one of the leading airlines in North America. In recent years, the airline has conducted a number of internal profit improvement initiatives that have delivered mixed results. Now their management team is seeking external advice. Their question: How should we grow our profits over the next three years? They have invited her to present her recommendations in two weeks.

Cheryl has worked on several similar initiatives. She could easily build a story, sharing her top ten recommendations but how valuable would a generalized approach be to her client? Having never worked with this airline before, she has little knowledge of what has already been tried, what has succeeded, and what has failed. Presenting content that they know already would add little value.

Cheryl responds to the invitation. *"I'd be glad to present to your executives in two weeks, but could we set up a short meeting this week? I'd like to ask a few questions to make sure that my presentation will accurately address your needs."* A 30-minute pre-meeting is agreed with three members of the executive team, two days later.

The content of a good story is not curated by guesswork. You will need to align with the needs of your audience first.

Considering her approach to this pre-meeting, Cheryl now has a choice. She could go in with a blank sheet of paper and simply ask questions based on her experience. But instead, she decides to apply a hypothesis-driven co-creation technique that will increase the amount of relevant input collected and pinpoint the direction needed to build the right story. This technique is known as a "logic tree."

What is a logic tree?

A logic tree is a tool that will help you to frame a problem and define the content and priorities required to address the needs of your audience. The approach involves two steps:

Step 1: Brainstorming to build the tree: A structured brainstorming session is performed, either by yourself or with your team, to identify the content that you plan to cover in your story. Driven by the vision that you have defined and your understanding of your audience, the logic tree diagram is built based on your experience in the subject domain. It's a hypothesis: An initial idea that has not been validated with the audience yet.

Step 2: Validation and the collection of input: Bring the tree to a meeting with a selection of key stakeholders from your target audience. Validate your ideas, collect feedback, capture additional inputs, and establish priorities. You can then fine-tune your approach and build a story that *both* leverages your domain expertise and accurately addresses the expectations of the receiving audience.

Step 1: Building the logic tree

Cheryl begins brainstorming to create her logic tree:

1. She starts by noting down the problem to be addressed, "Low profit."

2. Taking a top-down approach, based on her experience, she notes down the main areas that should be covered to address the problem. These areas become the main branches of her logic tree. In this case, two areas are

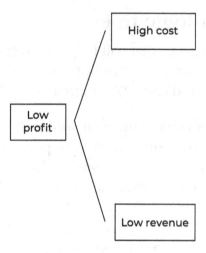

Figure 3.1: Logic tree: Main branches

identified: "*High cost*," where she plans to address costs that could be reduced or avoided to contribute to improved profit, and "*Low revenue*," where she plans to consider revenues that could be improved, illustrated in Figure 3.1.

If these areas are addressed well in her story, she believes that her client should be satisfied. The number of branches defined on the tree can vary depending on the issue itself, usually up to five in total.

3. Now brainstorming at a more detailed level, she breaks down these branches to identify the *individual elements* that should be considered within each area.

Based on her industry experience she notes down nine specific elements under cost, and seven elements under revenue, some of which are broken down one additional level.

Her hypothesis, illustrated in Figure 3.2, is now complete. If she had no further opportunity to engage with her client, this is the content that she would have planned to analyze and then build into her story.

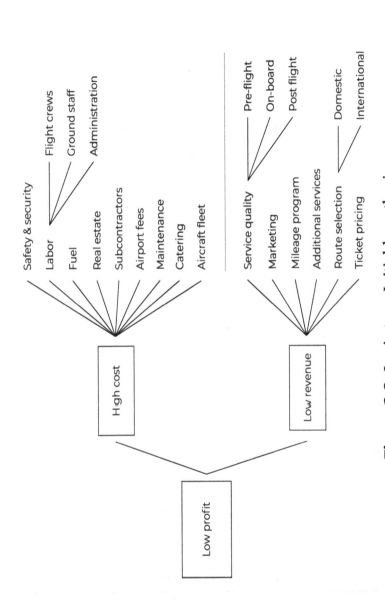

Figure 3.2: Logic tree: Initial hypothesis

Step 2: Using the logic tree in a co-creation session

Cheryl has secured a 30-minute meeting with three of the airline's executives. Rather than traveling to their head office for this short session, a 3-hour flight from her home location, she sets up a virtual meeting and shares the logic tree diagram on-screen for validation and the collection of feedback.

She begins by introducing the method: A simple way to break down the problem, obtain feedback, and to better understand their needs and priorities. She explains:

> *The content shown here is based on my experience. But I would like to tailor the approach to the needs of your business. Perhaps some of the items can be eliminated if they are not of interest to you, and we can agree on your priorities at a more detailed level.*

She walks the stakeholders through each part of the tree and asks them to comment. They provide the following feedback, beginning with the cost branch:

- They have already made significant investments in safety and security. No further action is required.

- There is a specific concern about labor costs related to their administrative organization. Recommendations would be welcomed in this area.

- Some other elements such as fuel, real estate, subcontractor services, airport fees, maintenance, and catering have recently been overhauled.

- They are under pressure to replace an aging fleet of Boeing 767 aircraft which are unpopular with customers and expensive to maintain. A study to identify a replacement is of interest.

Working on-screen, Cheryl marks this feedback directly onto the tree, circling areas of interest and striking out those deemed unnecessary.

> **Marking feedback onto the diagram in real time is important. You are agreeing on the content that will be addressed in the story. It's important to make sure that everyone is on the same page.**

The discussion continues to the revenue branch:

- The executives say that they are satisfied with feedback on service quality, but Cheryl catches their attention by raising a project that she recently completed concerning personalization of the on-board experience. They change their opinion and ask her to include this area in her recommendations.

- There is an interest in exploring "additional services," in particular value-added services that could be used to grow revenue, such as limousine transfers and door-to-door baggage delivery.

- They express interest in an additional area "partnerships" that was not included in Cheryl's hypothesis. Cheryl simply adds it to the diagram.

At the end of the session, Cheryl asks the executives to prioritize the areas that have been highlighted. This will help to determine the amount of effort that should be invested in each, and the weight that it should carry in the final story.

Personalization of on-board services scores priority #1, the fleet replacement program #2, administration costs #3, value-added services #4, and partnerships as #5. The finalized logic tree is illustrated in Figure 3.3.

The meeting conclusion

Presented with a loosely specified problem statement Cheryl brought in a hypothesis in the form of a logic tree, outlining her intended content for this story, that was subsequently reshaped during the meeting.

Several of the proposed elements were eliminated; one element was challenged, discussed, and then accepted, and an additional unforeseen element was added. Priorities were agreed and additional inputs were collected.

Cheryl is satisfied with this outcome. The exercise has been instrumental in framing the problem and defining the content strategy for her story. She feels certain that if she builds a story around the highlighted elements, her audience will find it valuable. If this exercise had not been performed, she would have spent time analyzing and creating content that would have been of little interest to the audience when presented.

Good stories are not built by guesswork. As a storyteller, you may be an expert in your field but you're not a mind-reader. The ability to frame the problem is therefore an essential skill.

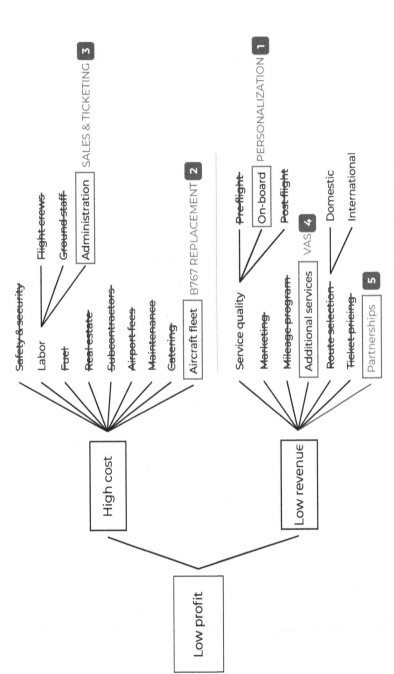

Figure 3.3: Logic tree including stakeholder feedback

The airline executives leave the meeting feeling confident that their needs have been understood and that the presentation in two weeks will be valuable.

Practical tips for running a co-creation session

A co-creation session is a powerful way to align on the precise needs and interests of your key stakeholders before building a story. Some stakeholders do not articulate their needs clearly or may require guidance in defining them. When running this type of session:

- **Be ready to introduce the method:** Your stakeholders may not have seen the logic tree method before. Be ready to introduce it, clearly in few words:

  A simple way for us to break down the issue, agree on the content to be addressed, and obtain additional inputs.

- **Take a navigation check point:** Start the process of validation by taking a check point at the branch level. *"These are the different areas that we have considered. Do you agree? Is anything missing? And which areas are most important to you?"* Discuss the branches in order of interest, not necessarily from top to bottom. This will ensure that the most important areas are discussed first.

- **Ask, don't present:** Remember that the tree is essentially a list of questions. Don't fall into the trap of presenting all the details on each branch and then asking for feedback. Your stakeholders should be doing most of the talking.

- **Use the visual nature of the technique:** Rather than discussing each item individually, leverage the visual nature of the method. *"Take a look at the items on this branch. Does anything stand out to you, or is anything redundant?"* Guide your stakeholders to read the items on each branch and take on some of the workload. This triggers a proactive response and is more time-efficient.

- **Co-creation is a two-way dialogue:** Your stakeholders may be keen to eliminate an element, but if you strongly disagree, you might need to challenge them, with good arguments. Cheryl demonstrated this in the discussion with her client about the on-board experience. Co-creation should bring together the knowledge of both parties to make good decisions. Your insights may be needed to shape the story as much as theirs.

- **Mark clear feedback and take good notes:** Mark feedback onto the tree in real time. Circle items for inclusion and strike out those that are not of interest. Use a dotted line notation for "possible" items that need further investigation before a decision can be made.

- **At the end, agree on priorities:** Remember to prioritize the elements that have been highlighted at the end of the session. You can then decide how much effort to invest in each one when you develop your story. If many elements have been highlighted, it may be wiser to focus on the few most important, initially.

Case study: SmartStream

The Jensen team applies the same approach to their assignment for improving SmartStream's billing capabilities, also a somewhat open-ended question.

They bring three team members together to conduct a brainstorming session and to build a logic tree: Justin Phillips, a senior technical expert; Jessica Yu, an experienced program manager; and Ross Wagner, a junior analyst. The team members have been selected based on their knowledge of the technology industry and the billing domain.

Their tree is structured around four main branches:

1. *The business needs* that SmartStream should aim to address with new billing capabilities.
2. *Related processes* that will require attention.
3. *New system functionalities* that will be required.
4. *Architecture options* to be evaluated, moving forward.

Based on their knowledge of SmartStream's needs and their industry experience, they identify six elements related to business needs, four in the process area, seven targeted functionalities and two architectural approaches. Their logic tree is illustrated in Figure 3.4.

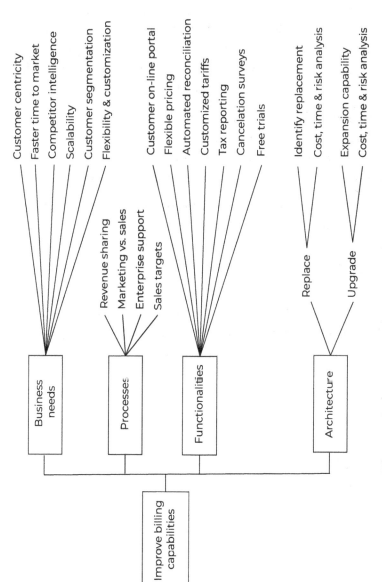

Figure 3.4: Jensen's logic tree for SmartStream

They schedule a meeting with two of SmartStream's executives, Kristina Lassen (CMO) and Nils Mortensson (CTO), which they plan to run as a co-creation session to collect feedback. The items on Figure 3.4 are validated, items of interest and are highlighted, those not of interest are eliminated.

The executives agree with Jensen's assessment of the key business needs to be addressed, but state that they already have sufficient competitor intelligence and a well-developed customer segmentation strategy.

Processes are not front of mind, but Jensen reminds them that they have an imminent requirement to implement new revenue-sharing models with content providers. A new process will be required for this.

Four of the specific billing functionalities that Jensen has listed are deemed to be most important, others are deferred to a later date. And the stakeholders agree on the two architectural approaches to be evaluated. At the end of the discussion, the highlighted items are prioritized.

The finalized logic tree, illustrated in Figure 3.5, gives Jensen the direction that they need to perform the right analysis to build the right story to meet the needs of their audience.

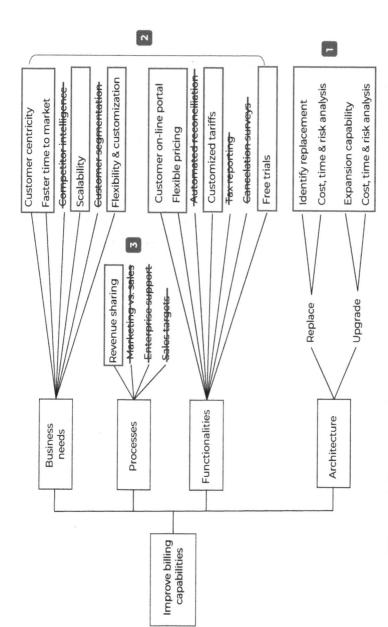

Figure 3.5: Jensen's logic tree after feedback from SmartStream

Experience from the field

A vice-president in technology sales shared his experience of using this approach for the first time:

> *"I tried using the logic tree in a meeting with one of our clients last week. It's a client that is not usually very good at explaining what they want. They were a little surprised because they had never seen anything like it before. But they opened up and shared their thoughts and opinions. It's started a discussion that we've been trying to get going for weeks. They seemed to enjoy the session and they've asked us for another meeting next week to talk more."*

A product innovation manager in the automotive industry commented on the applicability of the approach internally within her organization:

> *"I see a lot of good applications for this approach within our organization. Sometimes I ask one of our teams to prepare an internal report on a potential design opportunity. After two weeks I receive a draft for review, but it's not exactly what I had in mind. I ask them to make changes and that takes another week. If we followed a process like this, we would get it right, first time."*

Chapter summary

- In business, many of the issues that we are required to build stories to address are vaguely specified from the outset.

- We may need to frame the problem more clearly before we can build a story to accurately address the issue.

- The logic tree is a technique that can help to achieve this and involves a two-step process.

  - First, create a logic tree diagram based on your knowledge of the problem domain, and the content that you would plan to address in the story.

  - Second, conduct a co-creation session with a subset of your stakeholders. Use the session to agree on what should be in focus and what is irrelevant. Align on priorities.

- Remember that co-creation is a two-way process. It should combine your insights and the opinions of your stakeholders to make good decisions.

- The outcome will provide you with the content strategy and direction needed to build a story to accurately address the needs of your audience.

Next steps

Reflect on your personal case study. Build a logic tree that lists the areas and elements that you plan to cover in your story. Then validate it with members of the receiving audience, capture their inputs and priorities, and refine your areas of focus.

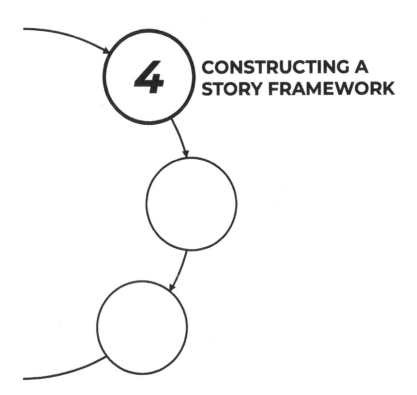

4 CONSTRUCTING A STORY FRAMEWORK

Building a skyscraper begins with a robust architectural blueprint. Constructing a story framework works in much the same way.

CHAPTER FOUR

CONSTRUCTING A STORY FRAMEWORK

Constructing a story framework is the heart of the storytelling process. It's where you anchor your story, connect your key messages into a logical flow and create the supporting structures needed to make it robust and defensible.

The framework is created by combining a series of logical arguments that may include facts, data, and the findings from analysis as well as less tangible elements such as experience, opinions, and emotional biases. We will introduce two principal approaches used to build these arguments, each quite different in nature but with an important role to play.

Once created, the framework is documented in the form of a one-page *story blueprint* that can be translated into whichever delivery format needed: a conversation, keynote speech, document, or presentation. The blueprint makes elaborating the story, crafting the narrative and designing support material a more straightforward and efficient process.

Building logical arguments: deductive and inductive methods

There are two types of argument predominantly used in storytelling: the deductive and inductive methods.

A deductive argument embodies horizontal logic

A deductive argument embodies the process of sequential or *horizontal logic*, taking the audience on a logical journey from starting point to conclusion. It is primarily used to ensure that a story has a robust and logical flow. Let's examine its use with a simple example (Figure 4.1).

Figure 4.1: Deductive argument

A deductive argument has three principal characteristics:

1. **It must be anchored with a solid starting point:** To take an audience on a journey, you need to start from the same place. If you are not aligned from the outset, you won't get very far. This makes the choice of starting point important. In practice, it is usually:

    a. A *fact*, something that is provable or observable.

    b. A *point of firm agreement*, something that you know that you and your audience already agree upon.

    The starting point in our example, "it is raining," would need to be anchored with some evidence (e.g., by looking out of the window and observing the rain) for the starting point to be solid.

2. **The argument ends with a firm conclusion or call-to-action:** If all the premises in the argument hold true, so should the conclusion.

3. **Each premise brings the audience one step closer to the conclusion:** The argument takes the audience on a step-by-step, logical journey from point A to point B.

The deductive method is a powerful tool in storytelling. It can follow different logical paths from starting point to conclusion depending on the context, all of which satisfy the above criteria. Some examples are illustrated in Figure 4.2.

The number of premises in the argument can vary

While the examples above illustrate arguments comprising four premises and a conclusion, this can vary.

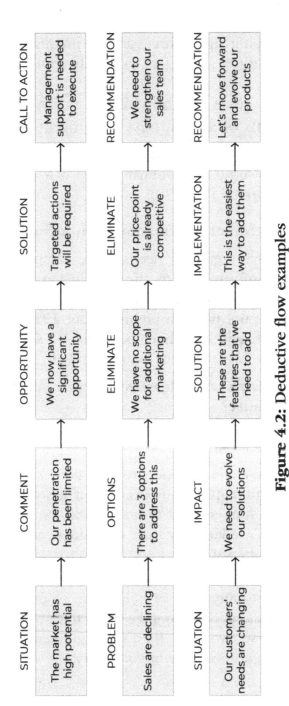

Figure 4.2: Deductive flow examples

Arguments built upon three or five premises are also common. The rule of 4 +/− 1 generally applies.

Two safety tests can be used to verify the strength of a deductive argument

These tests should always be applied to ensure that the argument is sufficiently robust before it is included in the framework of a story:

1. **Has all relevant information been included?**

   A deductive argument needs to be complete. If any relevant information to the conclusion is missing, the argument can be overturned. In our example, you might not have an umbrella, but a raincoat. The conclusion will no longer be valid. Be sure that all relevant information has been included.

2. **Can we prove, or at least reasonably substantiate, each premise?**

   A deductive argument must be built on solid premises, usually backed up by evidence or analysis. It's like a chain. If one premise fails, so does the whole argument. In our example if it stops raining, if you no longer need to go outside, or if there are umbrellas available for loan, then the conclusion will no longer be valid.

These are the only two ways, in logic, to overturn this type of argument. If you build a deductive argument and it passes these two tests, then the argument should be robust enough to include in your story.

The inductive argument embodies vertical logic

Deductive arguments work well in situations where we have solid information available to justify each premise, but do not easily accommodate subjective information or details that are easy for the audience to dispute.

In these situations, a second type of argument is available: the inductive argument. Embodying the process of *vertical logic*, the argument aggregates good and different reasons to illustrate that something is very likely to be true. The better the reasoning included, the more likely the audience will be to accept the conclusion.

While a deductive argument embodies an analytical style, an inductive argument embodies a more persuasive style. Let's examine its characteristics using the example in Figure 4.3.

In our example the assertion "You won't like the film" is backed by three reasons: "Megan didn't like it," "The reviews have been bad," and "You rarely enjoy action films."

Figure 4.3: Inductive argument

Consider the following criteria when building an inductive argument:

1. **Base the argument on three to five premises:** These should be good and different reasons that support your conclusion. Including more than five reasons reduces the focus of your argument. In this case, consider regrouping your information and focus on what is most important.

2. **Has all relevant information been included?** Once again, all relevant information must be included.

3. **Are the reasons aligned with the interests of your audience?** Think about the interests, priorities, and decision-making criteria of your audience. This is what will make the argument compelling. If they don't care about a premise, it is redundant.

An inductive argument is easier to defend, making it useful at the detailed level

The inductive argument may not provide as solid a conclusion as the deductive method but it is easier to defend. If a premise fails, perhaps Megan changes her mind and says that the film wasn't so bad after all, then the argument will be weakened but not necessarily overturned. It has two other assertions to lean on. In practice, each reason will carry a different weight and level of certainty, something that should be considered when building this type of argument.

The inductive method can support both solid and subjective information

The deductive method requires each statement to be solid for the argument to hold true, whereas an inductive argument can accommodate a mix of solid and subjective statements. "Megan didn't like it" is a subjective statement yet can still add momentum to the case being made.

Order the supporting reasons by priority

It's good practice to list the most important reasons first to capture the attention of the audience.

Inductive arguments can be used to rationalize pros and cons

If an assertion in your story relies on the weighing of pros and cons, the inductive method can be useful.

If the conclusion of the argument *supports* an assertion positively, it is usual to begin with the cons and to follow with the pros, as illustrated in Figure 4.4. While in this example there are more pros than cons, this will not always be the case. The weight of each reason plays

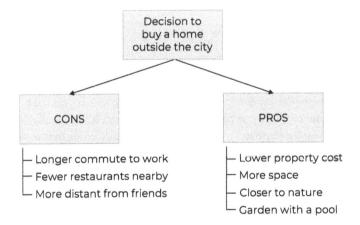

Figure 4.4: Inductive argument supporting a positive assertion

an important role. Three strong, compelling pros could outweigh five less significant cons.

The weighing of pros and cons can play an important role in the storytelling that we do in business.

When building an argument that positively supports an assertion, should we underplay the cons completely? Usually not. We live in an imperfect world and when an argument becomes too one-sided, it becomes less credible. Research has shown that including a small dose of negative detail in an otherwise positive description creates a more positive impact. This is referred to as the "blemishing effect."[1]

If the conclusion of the argument *negates* an assertion, it is usual to begin with the pros and to follow with the cons (Figure 4.5).

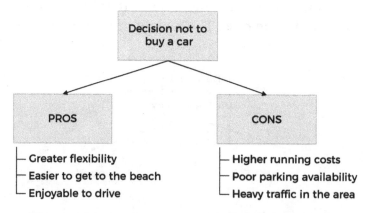

Figure 4.5: Inductive argument supporting a negative assertion

The methods can be combined to build the framework of a story

The framework of a story utilizes a mix of deductive and inductive arguments that can be visualized in the form of a pyramid, organizing information into a logical hierarchy (Figure 4.6).

The pyramid is divided into three layers:

The first layer is the concluding statement of your story. Typically, a recommendation or call-to-action.

The second layer forms the key argument: the backbone of the story. This generally requires the most thought and effort in preparation. It will determine how the rest of the content in the story is organized.

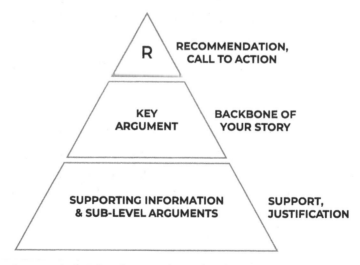

Figure 4.6: The hierarchy of information in a story

The third layer contains supporting information, based on research, inputs, and analysis, supported by additional arguments.

Each layer in the pyramid is supported by the one beneath it. The logical connection of these layers results in a coherent story. Let's explore the practical application of this idea by returning to our SmartStream case study.

Case study: SmartStream

The co-creation exercise performed with Smart-Stream's executives provided the Jensen team with the input and direction required to steer their analysis.

Three weeks have been spent with a focus on:

1. Changes in the market and competitive landscape.
2. Understanding the current systems already in place.
3. Evaluation of SmartStream's options, moving forward.

Having concluded their analysis, the Jensen team intends to recommend that SmartStream upgrades its existing billing system rather than replacing it. This will be seen as controversial by some members of the management team who have already stated a preference for a new system.

The Jensen team has 10 days to build a story around their recommendation and to prepare two deliverables:

- A written report
- A presentation

Building a story for the SmartStream case

Recommendation

The team starts by noting down the recommendation that they plan to deliver: "Upgrade billing system." This forms the top layer of their pyramid.

Key argument

They then build their key argument, shown in Figure 4.7.

- The argument is anchored with a solid starting point: a fact or a point of firm agreement, something that will resonate with the audience and reflect their reality. They use SmartStream's ambitions relative to the issue at hand, a need to secure their leading position. This has been reiterated by their client in several discussions.

- For the achievement of this, they require new functional capabilities in their billing system as well as additional scalability to deal with subscriber growth. This is added as the second step in the argument.

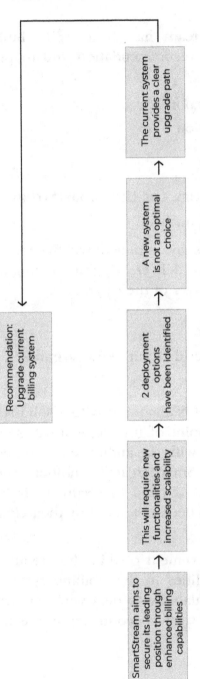

Figure 4.7: Recommendation and key argument for SmartStream

- They introduce the idea that two different deployment options have been evaluated: either to replace or to upgrade.

- They explain that their analysis has concluded that a new system is unfavorable at the current time.

- Their findings indicate, however, that the current system offers a clear upgrade path.

- Hence the recommendation to move forward and upgrade the current billing system.

The key argument is complete. A deductive argument has been used to provide a logical flow (Figure 4.8). It has a starting point that anchors the story in the context, ends with a clear recommendation, and every step in the argument brings the audience closer to the recommendation. Just by reading these statements an observer would understand the overall message delivered by the story.

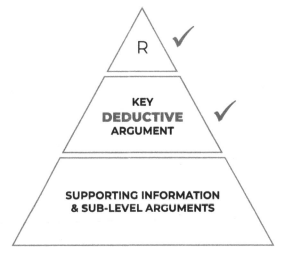

Figure 4.8: A deductive argument as a key argument

For the deductive argument, remember that two safety tests must be performed:

• Has all relevant information been included?

At the high level, the team is confident:

• Can we prove, or at least reasonably substantiate, each premise?

The premises must be solid. If any one of them is disputed, then the deductive chain will be broken and the recommendation will be overturned.

To support each of the premises, the team adds supporting information based on their analysis, shown in Figure 4.9.

Supporting information and arguments

The first supporting argument describes SmartStream's business drivers for this initiative. They return to the audience understanding template prepared earlier (Chapter 2) and use it to complete this information, ensuring that the story will resonate with the executives.

The second supporting argument homes in on the specific needs captured. The team uses the output of their co-creation session (Chapter 3) to complete these details. The validation that was performed in the session ensures alignment on these points.

The remaining supporting arguments are based on the findings of their analysis. These are inductive arguments based on three to five reasons to support corresponding statements in the key argument.

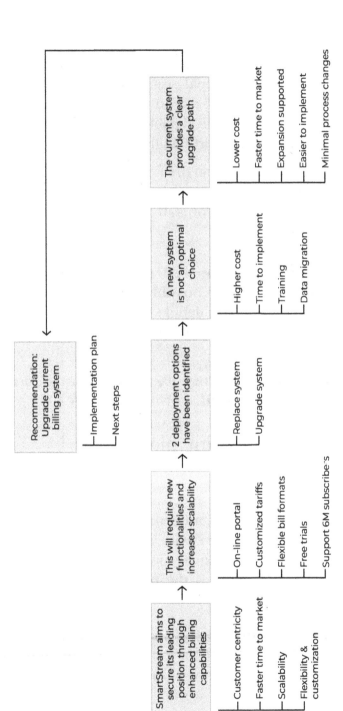

Figure 4.9: Addition of supporting information and sub-level inductive arguments

- If they are challenged on the second statement: "Are new capabilities and additional scalability really required?," they will respond, "Yes, due to the need for an on-line portal, customized tariffs, flexible bill formats, free trials and the ability to support 6 million subscribers."

- If they are challenged on the fourth premise: "Is a new system really unfeasible?," they will respond, "Yes, due to cost, time, training for staff on and significant data migration efforts."

Inductive arguments are well suited to provide this support as it is not always possible to gain full agreement with an audience at the detailed level (Figure 4.10). If one item comes into dispute, it will not necessarily be as problematic.

The framework of the story, documented in the format of the one-page *blueprint* shown is complete.

The story blueprint plays an important role

The blueprint provides a mechanism to ensure that the story is well anchored, audience-centric, has a clear (deductive) flow, together with strong (inductive) supporting structures. A deductive key argument supported by inductive arguments is the most common arrangement used in storytelling.

- **It organizes information into a clear hierarchy:** From recommendation or call-to-action to the key argument and supporting information. This is essential as the stories that we tell in business should be scalable. If you meet one of the executives in the

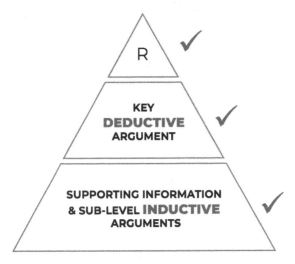

Figure 4.10: Inductive arguments as
supporting arguments

elevator and you are asked to give an update, you
should be able to summarize your story in one minute by narrating only the key argument.

- **It saves time:** Show the blueprint to colleagues and
obtain feedback on the flow and content before spend-
ing hours translating it into a document or presentation. This is more efficient than asking them to review
a 20-page document later in the process.

Building a story blueprint is an exercise in structured
thinking and logic. It is an iterative process. Don't be
dissuaded if you find that it requires several revisions
before you are satisfied with the flow and supporting
structures. You are training your storytelling muscles
and improving the quality of the result! Two additional
examples taken from different industries are provided
in Figures 4.11 and 4.12.

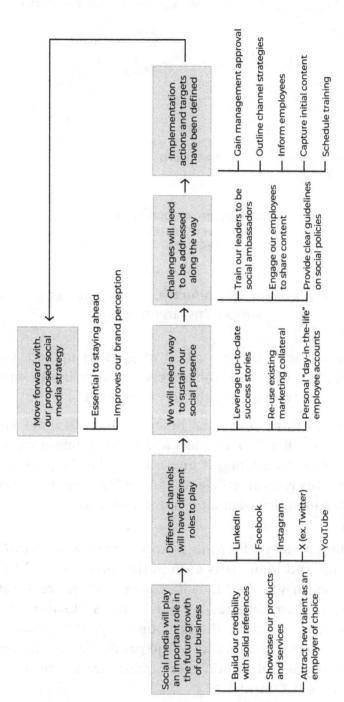

Figure 4.11: The presentation of a social media strategy

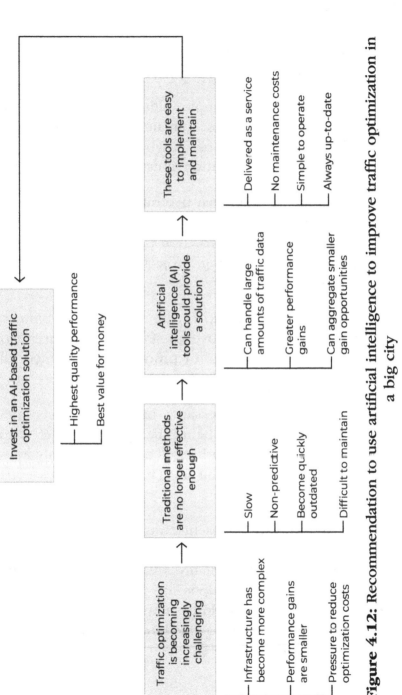

Figure 4.12: Recommendation to use artificial intelligence to improve traffic optimization in a big city

In some cases, an inductive argument can be used as the key argument

The majority of stories employ a deductive key argument but in some specific cases an inductive argument can be used. The most notable is when preparing a status report or status presentation, illustrated in Figure 4.13.

The example assumes that five different KPIs (key performance indicators) areas are being reported. If you are running a building construction project, these might be building supplies, staffing, project progress, client relationships, and safety.

For each area at the top of the hierarchy a summary statement explains the overall status of each area. For example, "Safety: Review of procedures is needed following two accidents this month."

Beneath are the key messages based on the reported data and detailed KPIs being measured for each area. The inductive format works well as there are only loose dependencies between the areas rather than an essential logical flow.

At the monthly progress meeting if your safety manager says. "I can only join the first 20 minutes of this meeting. Could I present my area first?," changing the order in which the sections are presented should not be a problem. This would be more difficult in a deductive arrangement due to the horizontal dependencies between the parts of the story.

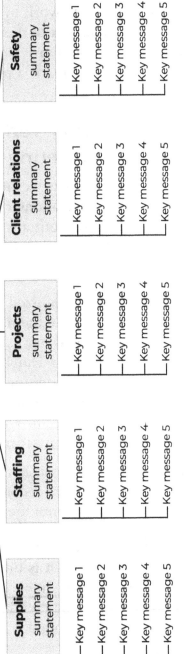

Figure 4.13: Use of inductive key argument in status reporting

Having designed the framework of your story, the hard work is done. The remainder of this chapter will discuss how the blueprint can be translated into a verbal delivery of the story, a document, or a presentation.

Presenting the story verbally, in a conversation or meeting

Much of the storytelling that we do in business is performed in meetings, conversations, or over the telephone. This is generally done without any visual support material and is a test of the ability to verbally articulate a story with clarity.

The story blueprint has organized your ideas and you will be ready to communicate them in a structured, logical format. While you would not usually share the blueprint with your audience, it can be useful to keep it close to hand during the discussion, as an instrument of guidance as you navigate through the discussion.

Conclusion first or conclusion last?

When delivering the story you have a choice – should you present your conclusion, recommendation, or call-to-action first or leave this until the end?

Both approaches are valid. The advantage of presenting your conclusion first is that it is time-efficient and enables you to get to the point quickly. But if you are presenting a controversial recommendation that is likely to shock your audience, you might want to leave it to the end. Hearing the way that the story builds up may make the recommendation easier for your audience to accept.

Checkpoints keep you in synch with your audience

Delivering a story is not about reciting a script, but rather taking your audience on a journey. You need to make sure that you keep them with you on that journey.

The best way to achieve this is by taking checkpoints after each step as you deliver the story. "Do you agree? Any questions so far?" This avoids the dilemma of losing your audience and having to go back three steps to resolve a point lacking clarity.

Try to secure acceptance at each stage

Gaining acceptance from an audience is an incremental process that builds gradually as your story progresses.

As you deliver your story, you are likely to encounter differences of opinion which will need to be addressed. Even if these differences cannot be resolved, they should always be taken on board. If you brush off a conflicting opinion and simply move on, you are likely to lose the interest of the individuals concerned.

Show a willingness to listen and seek to understand. "That's an interesting view, could you elaborate more?" Decide whether to contest or to accept a difference of opinion. "In my experience, I have found the opposite to apply . . ."

Anticipate likely questions and be ready to answer them

Senior executives are often more interested in how well you answer their questions than in the material that you present. Handling questions is therefore an important part of the task and preparation plays an important role. Anticipate the questions that your audience is likely to ask and prepare good answers.

Translating the blueprint into a document

From the story blueprint it is quite easy to define the structure of a document or report.

The executive summary

The key argument is elaborated into an executive summary, where each main statement becomes a paragraph, illustrated in Figure 4.14.

Executive summary: SmartStream

SmartStream aims to secure its leading position through the introduction of enhanced billing capabilities. This is a critical and timely move, given current market conditions with a focus on customer centricity, faster time to market, scalability to address a growing customer base, and the ability to provide billing flexibility and customized offerings.

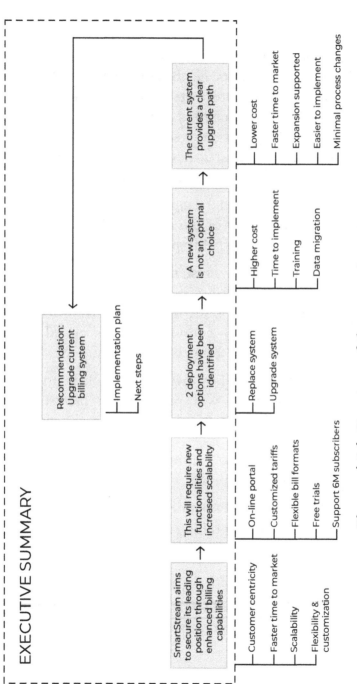

Figure 4.14: Structure of the executive summary

The target architecture will require functionality and processes to support an on-line portal. SmartStream will need to offer its customers customized tariffs and flexible billing formats to compete effectively, particularly in the business segment. Free trials will be essential to boost new service introduction, and our estimates suggest a need to support up to six million subscribers over the next three years.

This challenge could be approached in two ways: either a replacement of the current billing system or an upgrade of the existing platform.

Implementing a new system is not optimal at this time due to the high associated cost, an implementation time of 16 months, the need to train staff on a new system, and complexities associated with migrating data from the existing system.

The current system, however, offers a clear upgrade path. This solution will provide the fastest time to market, estimated at 6 months, and the needed expansion can be supported technically. This implementation will not be complex and minimal process changes will be required.

Hence our recommendation to move forward and upgrade the existing billing system.

An executive summary is an important part of a report and is the only part that some executives will ever read. Don't write a few paragraphs of vague introductory text, rather present the high-level message of your story and use the executive summary to gain their buy-in.

Chapters and sub-sections

Each premise in the key argument will represent a chapter within the document, while the supporting reasons contained in the second-level inductive arguments become sections within each chapter, illustrated in Figure 4.15.

With the addition of explanatory content under each section heading, whether a few paragraphs of text, charts, figures, or diagrams, the story is documented in a format that is well argued at every point.

Use meaningful titles

While the items on the story blueprint are generally written in shortened format, the titles for the chapters and sections in a document should be meaningful, displaying clear messages that tell the story. It is common practice to elaborate each one into a full sentence (including a verb).

A poor practice example:

Chapter 1	Enhancing billing capabilities
1.1	Customer centricity
1.2	Faster time to market

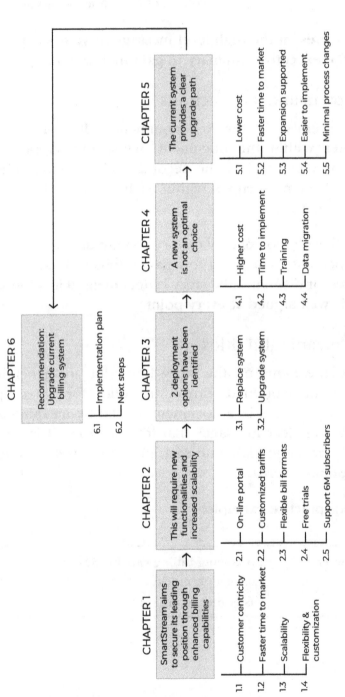

Figure 4.15: Overall document structure

A good practice example:

Chapter 1	SmartStream aims to secure its leading position through enhanced billing capabilities
1.1	Customer centricity is a cornerstone of the company's strategy
1.2	Faster time to market will be essential to compete effectively
1.3	Scalability will be an enabler to future business growth
1.4	Flexible billing formats and customized offerings will attract the enterprise segment

The reader should be able to skim through a document, reading only the titles and understand the essence of the story.

Employ an approachable writing style

Employ a writing style that is approachable and not excessively formal to increase ease of comprehension. Think of how the chapters of this book apply this idea, intended to make the reader feel that they are being coached through each point, supported by examples.

Translating the blueprint into a presentation

The blueprint also makes the creation of presentation slides a straightforward process.

First, decide the target length of the presentation and the amount of detail to be included. The simplest format for our SmartStream example would be a presentation of six main content slides, where:

- Each premise in the key argument is translated into a presentation slide;

- The wording of each statement is elaborated into a meaningful slide title;

- The supporting (inductive) points are expanded into the content of each slide.

If a more detailed presentation is required, each statement could be expanded into a group of slides instead of a single slide, illustrated in Figure 4.16.

In this example the blueprint has been translated into 14 presentation slides. Consideration has been given to the level of detail required for each part of the story, some parts requiring more elaboration than others. Presentations created without a blueprint often lack this discipline. A presentation that should have required only 14 slides can easily end up at a length of 20 slides.

Design effective presentation slides

Well-designed presentation slides should be clear, attractive, well synchronized with the key messages in your story, and should accelerate the comprehension of the key messages by the audience.

Research suggests that when we listen to the presentation of information, we generally only recall 10% of the content, whereas if we listen and also see it represented

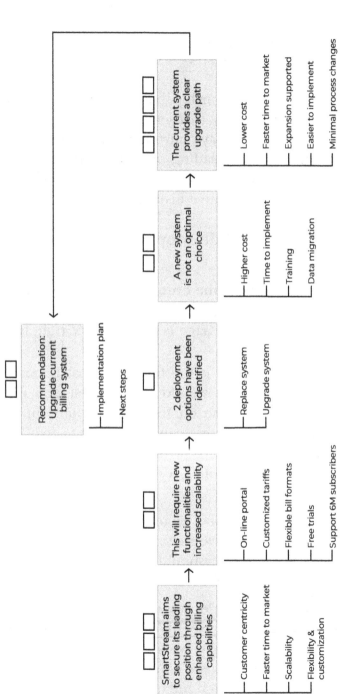

Figure 4.16: Jensen's presentation outline for SmartStream

visually, we retain as much as 65%. This is known as the "picture-superiority effect."[2]

Think about the relationship between the content on your slides and the way that you plan to narrate them. The narrative must always introduce new value, otherwise you will just be reading out your slides. In some cases, you might even omit certain details from the slides to include in your narrative instead.

The content of a slide represents a hierarchy of information

This hierarchy dictates the order in which the audience will read the information. It's therefore important to make sure that each message is placed at the right level:

1. **The slide title:** This is the first and most important message. Each slide should present just one main point. Everything else on the slide should support that point. The slide title can occupy up to two lines of text and has the largest font size, often 40pt. Just by reading the slide titles, a reader should be able to follow the storyline.

2. **A sub-title:** An optional element that can be used to add a second narrative message if needed. Together the title and sub-title should not occupy more than two lines. A smaller font size is used, often 32 pt.

3. **The body of the slide:** Try to keep the body of the slide as clear and visually appealing as possible. When using text in the body of the slide, avoid full sentences (unless you are citing a quotation). Shorten text by removing redundant words that do not diminish the meaning.

4. **A conclusion bar:** Another optional element summarizing the main take-away from the discussion on the slide or providing a linking statement to the next part of your story.

Titles play an important role in presentations

As in documents, titles play an important role in presentations.

> **If everything on your slides disappeared except the titles and sub-titles, a reader should still be able to follow the story.**

The application of this idea is very helpful to managers who need to review presentations quickly. They can just read the titles and then dive into the detail where needed.

The title of the agenda slide requires particular consideration

Avoid the use of *empty* slide titles such as "Agenda," "Overview," or "Contents" found at the beginning of many presentations. These titles sacrifice the opportunity to convey a meaningful message. Give your agenda a more meaningful title that encompasses the topics that you plan to cover in your story, such as "The scope of this study," "The opportunity to enter a new market," or "Our journey into new technologies."

Busy slides are a distraction to your audience

In storytelling, less is more. Beware of busy slides packed with information that distract your audience and make them unfocused. You need them to be focused, able to process everything that the speaker is saying while being guided through the structure of key points illustrated on the slide.

If a slide is overloaded with information, the key messages get lost as the audience "can't see the forest for the trees." It turns into a heap of information that lacks accompanying logic. In storytelling we always present information *with* logic so that we can control the interpretation of that information.

Arguably, some people like to use presentation programs to produce documents packed with information, a visually enhanced version of word processing. These slides should never be presented on-screen. Either create a light-version for on-screen presentation or use speaker notes for the additional information required by readers off-line.

Apply a consistent template and branding guide

The look and feel of presentation slides are essential to their role in communicating an effective message. Make sure that the layout is well structured, professional, consistent, and visually appealing.

If you are working for a large corporation, you should have access to a brand portal providing templates, guidelines, and resources such as pre-formatted slides that you can simply insert your content into. This will save you a lot of time and guarantees output of excellent quality. Every presentation should maintain the same corporate identity.

If you are working in a smaller organization or as an individual, there are a variety of template and slide repositories available in the public domain for purchase. These assets are generally inexpensive and offer excellent value considering their quality and ease of use.

Use animations wisely

Animation can be a very powerful tool when used wisely. When presenting a complex diagram you might want to use animation, bringing in different components as you talk about them. This keeps the audience with you and helps to avoid confusion.

Bullets on slides can also be animated, appearing one by one as you narrate them and preventing the audience from reading ahead. When animating bullets, make sure that you plan to talk over each one for at least a minute. If a new bullet is appearing every 10 seconds, it just becomes annoying!

Keep to the most basic styles of animation, having elements "appear" or "fade in" as you advance. Items flying in from the left and right or spinning around are perceived as juvenile in most business situations.

Case study: Jensen's presentation to SmartStream

With the above guidelines in mind, let's examine a shortened version of Jensen's final presentation to SmartStream.

The first slide includes a title and sub-title representing a hierarchy of information. The title is read first and then the sub-title.

Billing improvement study
Final recommendation for SmartStream

"Taking billing capabilities to the next level" is used as the title for the agenda slide, encapsulating the points that are to be covered in the presentation. The points on the agenda maintain a one-to-one relationship with the premises of the key argument in the story blueprint. The blueprint and agenda should always be synchronized.

Taking billing capabilities to the next level

- SmartStream's ambitions
- New billing capabilities
- Evaluation of two options
- Unsuitability of a new system
- Upgrade of the current system
- Recommendation

While the first topic on the agenda was documented as "SmartStream's ambitions," the title of the corresponding content slide has been elaborated to communicate a clear message, "SmartStream aims to maintain a leading position." A sub-title has also been used to elaborate the secondary message.

The body of the slide adopts a simple yet visual format. The main points to be covered concern customer centricity, time to market, scalability, and flexibility with supporting points at one level of detail lower than that shown on the story blueprint.

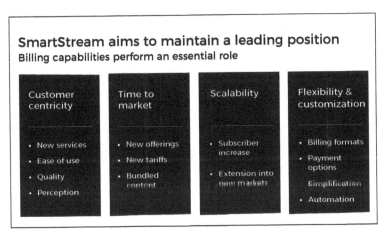

This slide also ultilizes a strong and meaningful title. Here sub-topics will be covered related to an on-line portal, customized tariffs, flexible bill formats, free trials, and capacity.

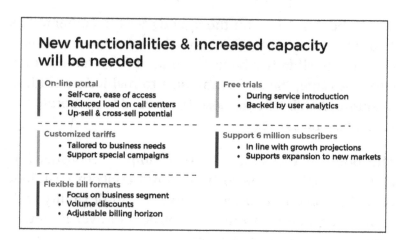

This slide visually outlines the two deployment options that have been identified.

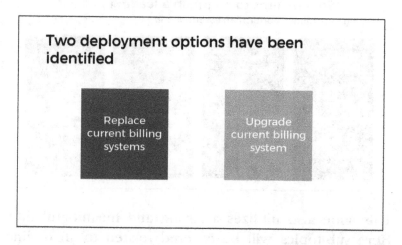

This slide, once again, utilizes both a title and subtitle. Big-number formats are used to communicate the key messages.

A new system would take 16 months to implement, cost 180M USD, 120 staff would require re-training and 30%

of the current pricing plans would have to be retired. The numbers communicate the most important messages.

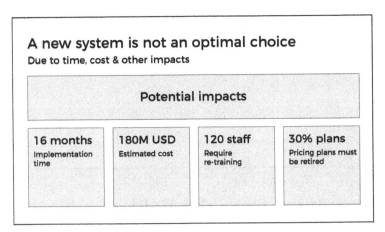

This slide lists the (inductive) reasons to proceed with an upgrade. At the bottom it utilizes an optional *conclusion bar*. The conclusion bar summarizes the key takeaway from the discussion on a slide.

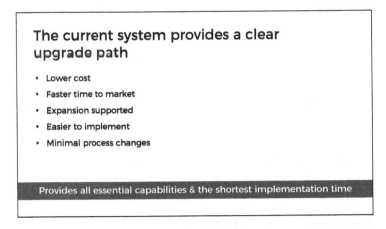

The final slide summarizes the recommendation and next steps.

Recommendation
Perform a system upgrade

- Define a. project time plan
- Secure project resources
- Identify dependencies
- Perform budget allocation

Experience from the field

A senior participant attending one of our storytelling training workshops at a technology corporation in Ireland commented:

> *"I feel that there's a common misconception that storytelling is purely about communicating. The ideas presented here prove that it's as much about organizing your thoughts and ideas before you communicate, as the communication itself."*

An industry analyst working in the healthcare industry in Germany commented:

> *"A big part of my job involves writing reports, which can be a tedious process. The story blueprint is excellent. It saves me so much time, directs my efforts, and eliminates a lot of frustration and wasted time."*

A marketing executive in North America commented:

"One of my greatest learnings is the importance of strong titles when telling a story in documents and presentations. Get the titles right and your most important messages will be received."

Chapter summary

- An effective story in business requires a robust logical framework.

- Two types of argument can be used to build the framework, deductive and inductive methods:

  - A deductive argument is used to create the backbone of the story and provide a logical flow.

  - The inductive method is used to create supporting arguments for the different parts of the story.

- Together they are used to formulate a one-page "story blueprint." This provides a good structure for verbal narration and can easily be translated into a document or presentation.

  - When preparing a report, the blueprint dictates the structure of the document, defining chapters and sections, or paragraphs for shorter document or email.

  - When preparing a presentation, the blueprint defines the agenda, flow, and supporting content structure.

- Titles play an important role and should convey the key messages in the story clearly.

Next steps

Using the guidelines presented in this chapter:

- Create a blueprint for the story that you are using as your personal case study.

- Design a set of presentation slides to elaborate your story.

Notes

1. "To sell is human." Daniel H. Pink, *Drive* (New York: Riverhead Books, 2013).
2. A.J.O. Whitehouse, M.T. Maybery, and K. Durkin, "The development of the picture-superiority effect." *British Journal of Developmental Psychology*, 24(4) (2006): 767–773.

5 PREPARING AN ENGAGING DELIVERY

A strong delivery requires structure, a compelling narrative and a well-thought-out interaction approach

CHAPTER FIVE

PREPARING AN ENGAGING DELIVERY

With the framework of your story in place, you are ready to prepare the content and the mechanics of your delivery. The approach will vary depending on your intended delivery format: presentation, keynote, or conversation.

A presentation is generally supported by some form or media such as slideware. A keynote, delivered to a larger audience, may use little or no support material and embodies minimal audience interaction. And a conversation, whether conducted in a meeting or informally at the coffee machine, is highly interactive and requires a greater level of flexibility as it takes on new directions as the discussion unfolds.

You will need to craft a strong narrative. This is where you bring your story to life, engage your audience, and win their support. The most accomplished storytellers use a rich selection of techniques to do this, some used spontaneously and others planned carefully in advance.

When delivering an important story the narrative must be a masterpiece.

This chapter shares a wide range of practical techniques used by some of the world's greatest storytellers to successfully engage their audiences. It is divided into five parts:

Part 1 examines the typical structure of a presentation delivery, divided into five phases, each of which has an important role to play.

Part 2 introduces some of the language constructions that can be incorporated into the narrative, improving its linguistic style, but moreover helping the audience to visualize and relate to the ideas presented.

Part 3 explores the underlying science of neurochemicals and the use of emotional triggers. These powerful tools will not only make your delivery more captivating but will enable you to influence the reactions of your audience and their willingness to support your cause.

Part 4 discusses the role of descriptive detail and the use of characters in a story, both highly applicable to the stories that we tell in business.

Part 5 demonstrates the use of the interaction techniques needed to solicit the inputs and agreements required to achieve your story's vision. It also introduces the use of alternative navigation approaches in response to unexpected shifts in audience priorities during your delivery.

Combine these techniques in a unique way to create your own narrative style.

Part 1: Mastering the five presentation phases

A presentation is typically divided into five phases, illustrated in Figure 5.1.

Opening words set the tone of your delivery

You have just stepped onto the stage. There is a moment of silence and anticipation. When you begin to speak, for the first 30 seconds you have the full attention of your audience. This is premium airtime that should be used wisely.

Your opening words should be profound and set the tone for the entire session. Don't waste them, as many do by thanking the audience or jumping straight into a speaker introduction.

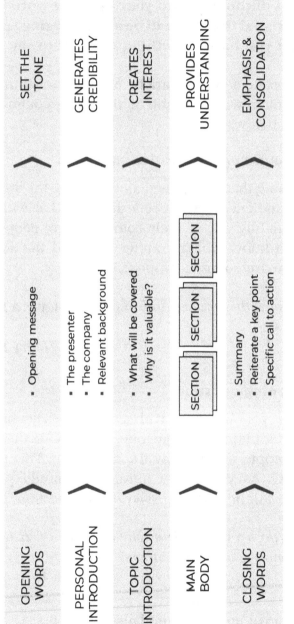

Figure 5.1: The five presentation phases

> **Put a lot of thought into your opening words. They should signal that you will be an interesting speaker and that you have something relevant to say.**

Skilled speakers use a variety of approaches to craft their opening words. Eight of the most common are described below.

1. A profound or provocative statement

Something that will immediately capture the attention of the audience. Introduce a dilemma that will move them slightly out of their comfort zone. People will want to know what's coming next and the solution that you are going to propose.

"A business that makes nothing but money is a poor business..."

—*Henry Ford*

2. An opening question

Provoke your audience with a question. The question should not be an obvious one, rather something that most people won't know the answer to. This evokes curiosity. As your story unfolds, it should provide either a full or partial answer to the question.

So how do we learn? And why do some of us learn things more easily than others?[1]

—*Dr. Lara Boyd*

A rhetorical question could also be used:

"Who wouldn't want an approach to build high-impact stories in a structured, reliable and repeatable way?"

—Samir Parikh

3. A quotation

A quotation can be powerful, provided its source is well known and seen to hold authority relative to the topic.

"It usually takes me more than three weeks to prepare a good impromptu speech."

—Mark Twain

4. An interesting statistic

Open with a surprising statistic that will resonate with the audience and capture their attention with relevance to your topic.

"Prince Philip, the Duke of Edinburgh and husband of Queen Elizabeth II, who died on April 9, 2021, made 22,219 solo public engagements over his lifetime."[2]

5. A build-up

A build-up that slowly reveals information either about yourself or your topic, creating curiosity.

"Something that very few people know is that. . ."

6. **A what-if scenario**

A scenario that provokes the audience to think and immerse themselves into the context of your topic.

"What if you could stop time whenever you wanted to? What if you could change one thing in your past?"

7. **An imagine scenario**

Present a scenario that brings the audience into an imaginary, parallel world. Let your story take them on a journey that starts in that place.

"Imagine being on an aircraft and hearing a big explosion as you climb through 3000ft. Imagine a plane full of smoke. Imagine an engine going clack, clack, clack. It sounds scary..."[3]

—Ric Elias

8. **A personal story of relevance to your topic**

Personal stories based on your own experience command a high level of attention from audiences.

"When I started in this industry 25 years ago, we used to deal mainly with engineering teams and technical people. But the telecoms industry has changed. Now we need to be ready to deal with a wider range of stakeholders, from marketing to operations and from top management to the working level."

Use one of the above techniques to create impactful opening words for your next presentation. Try out the

Figure 5.2: Characteristics of a credible speaker introduction

different methods, see which ones you find most effective, and consider them to be addition to your storytelling toolkit. Every presenter has their own unique style.

A well-crafted speaker introduction wins the listening ear of your audience

From your opening words transition smoothly into the next presentation phase: the speaker introduction. This is where you earn your position on the stage and win the listening ear of your audience.

An effective speaker introduction builds credibility by incorporating four essential characteristics (Figure 5.2).

Objective

A credible introduction is an objective one. Don't leap onto the stage, start beating your chest, and boasting your greatest achievements. Most people will just roll their eyes. A better style is one of simply presenting evidence. Present your credentials and let the audience make their own decision about who you are and the potential contributions that you can make.

Tangible

An introduction that is either vague or abstract is unlikely to be effective. Avoid fluffy statements such as "I bring a *broad experience* in the healthcare segment" or claim to be a "clinical *expert* in psychology." What exactly is a "broad experience"? And how should we define the subjective term "expert"? Use a tangible approach that quantifies expertise with qualifications, experience with numbers and makes specific references to relevant work that you have undertaken.

> *"I bring 12 years of experience in strategy consulting, specifically around mergers and acquisitions. I have just returned from a project in Mexico where we helped a client in the banking industry complete the acquisition of an insurance company."*

Relevant

Don't prepare a standard introduction of yourself that you recite the same way every time. Customize your approach relative to the audience and the situation at hand. Connect your skills and experience to the context. This usually means adjusting your points of emphasis and changing the examples and references included. Make your audience think "It will be interesting to listen to this person. Their insights and experience will be valuable."

Concise

A good speaker can deliver the maximum amount of meaning in the fewest number of words. Coupled with the prudent selection of vocabulary, this is a powerful attribute. Don't be too wordy. Keep it short and focus on what's most important.

Another powerful style is to turn your personal introduction into a story, explaining how your career has progressed over time and incorporating the facts that you want to include.

If everyone in the audience already knows your background relative to the topic, a speaker introduction may not be required. But in some cases, even a familiar audience may be unaware of the experience that you plan to draw upon and a short introduction can play an important role.

> *"You all know me well, but you probably don't know about the work that I did in the oil and gas industry 12 years ago. The approach to risk management there is much more scientific than the approach that we use in our projects. The ocean is a very hostile environment and if a risk turns into an issue, everyone on the rig could be killed. I'm going to draw on some of that experience in the strategies that I present today."*

When speaking at a conference or large event. it's likely that a host or moderator will introduce you. Beware, unprepared host introductions can be dangerous! Decide exactly what it is that you want the audience to know about you and brief the host in advance on the key points that they might want to include.

A good topic introduction presents a value proposition to the audience

The topic introduction connects your topic with your audience and gives them a reason to listen. Just because people showed up to the session doesn't mean that they are bought-in. What's in it for them? What problem are you going to solve for them?

Your ability to make this connection determines whether people will lean forward in their chairs hanging on your every word or sit back and check messages on their phones. Phrases such as, "*What I'm going to talk about today is. . .*", should definitely be avoided! They make no direct reference to any value for the audience.

> *"Today we are all under pressure to deliver faster and with higher quality. I'm going to share some of the lessons that we've learned, particularly from a recent case from the pharmaceuticals industry in Pittsburgh. I'll also share some valuable shortcuts that you can take and use in your projects straight away."*

The main body follows the structure of your story blueprint

The main body is where you tell your story and is where most of the work is done. It will follow the structure of your story blueprint, supported by a strong narrative and well-crafted audience interaction approach, discussed later in this chapter.

Closing words are often what people remember the most

It is often said that when presenting we deliver our key messages three times. In the topic introduction we tell people what we're going to tell them. In the main body we deliver our main messages. And in the summary, we tell people what we told them. But be careful with this idea, particularly when presenting to senior executives. They tend to have limited time, may be impatient, and dislike repetition.

> **As a speaker, you have a reasonable amount of control over the thought that you leave in the minds of your audience. With this in mind, pick your closing words carefully.**

For example:

- If you decide to end with a summary, don't just repeat what you have said already. Include a new angle or an interesting twist.

- If you want to reiterate a key point, do it clearly and emphatically. *"Thank you for attending the session today. If there's one thing that I would like you to take away from this, it is. . ."*

- And if you want to make a call to action, make it clear and be very specific. Tell people exactly what to do to if they want to act on your ideas.

Part 2: Linguistic structures: metaphors, analogies, and anecdotes

Metaphors, analogies, and anecdotes play an essential role in helping the audience to visualize a story, to relate to complex ideas, and, most of all, to make ideas more memorable. Make a habit of incorporating them in your narrative design.

Metaphors

A metaphor is a figure of speech that, for rhetorical effect, directly refers to one thing by mentioning another. It activates the imagination and improves the audience's ability to visualize an idea, while adding eloquence to your linguistic style. For example:

- I can't make it tonight. I'm buried in a sea of paperwork.
- You have just taken a weight off my shoulders.
- Let's get started. Time is money.
- This is not a solution, just a Band-Aid for the problem.
- Those guys in finance are just bean counters.
- And that was the final straw . . .
- She's coming in on the red eye from Boston tomorrow morning.

Analogies

Analogies are comparisons that help people relate to unfamiliar ideas. They bring clarity to complexity and can be very powerful in storytelling. After all, if the listeners do not understand an idea, they are unlikely to act on it.

Analogies help us to understand ideas that we know little about by associating them with things that we do know about. For example, you could say that the condition ADHD (attention deficit hyperactivity disorder) is like having a "Ferrari brain."

A technology consultant working in a large data center used this technique to explain the concept of transaction-based processing vs. batch processing to a new colleague who had little technical knowledge.

> *"Think of it this way," he said. "Transaction-based processing is like when someone comes to your door to deliver a package. They ring the doorbell, wait for a finite amount of time, probably 20–30 seconds. If you answer the door, they hand you the package and get you to sign a slip to confirm that the delivery has taken place. If you don't answer, they go away." That's how transaction-based processing works between our systems.*
>
> *"Every day when you come home from work you probably find a pile of letters on your door mat. You come in, make some coffee, and when you are ready, you read through them one by one. That's how batch processing works. It happens here during the night when we start a bill-run for our customers. The systems then read all the transaction records from the last month, one by one, and generate the bills."*

Anecdotes and personal examples

An anecdote is a short, amusing, or interesting story about a real incident or person that has relevance to the topic under discussion. Anecdotes are particularly memorable as humans crave the voice of experience and our brains are programmed to store them.

An anecdote could relate to a situation that you have heard or read about, or a personal event from your own career experience. Personal examples command a particularly high level of attention as they are unique. They are also easy for you to narrate as they are already ingrained in your memory. You are simply recounting a situation the way you remember it. For example:

- A sea captain giving a speech at a dinner tells a story about an incident in the Pacific, many years ago, where a large yacht came close to hitting a rock, and the reasons why it almost happened.

- A leader speaking at a company seminar talks about her first experience presenting to a large audience at a conference, how she felt nervous, and how she overcame it.

- A frequent traveler tells a colleague about a problem that occurred on a recent flight to Mexico City, describes the professionalism of the crew, and explains why, as a result, the airline has become his preferred choice.

Part 3: The underlying science of neurochemicals

Good storytellers can captivate their audiences and engage them in a way that wins and maintains their attention. But that doesn't happen by magic. There's an underlying science driven by neurochemicals that every good storyteller should understand and use to their advantage.

Neurochemicals drive the emotions of your audience, their reactions, the impact of your key messages and ultimately their willingness to act or support your cause.

The principal neurochemicals used in storytelling are:

- Dopamine
- Oxytocin
- Endorphin
- Cortisol
- Adrenaline.

The ability to build triggers into a story that stimulate the timing and release of these neurochemicals is a powerful skill.

Dopamine

Dopamine awakens our curiosity and makes us feel more focused and motivated. It activates the brain's learning systems and enables us to remember what we experience more easily and with greater accuracy.

High levels of dopamine mean that we are truly engaged. Our minds are unlikely to wander or become distracted. We feel compelled to follow the progress of a story and to find out what happens next.

The creators of TV shows are the masters of dopamine triggers, implemented through the creation of suspense and cliff-hangers. By leaving us with questions at the end of an episode, we are more likely to tune in and watch the next one.

A good story, irrespective of the topic, is therefore either subtly or emphatically dopamine-creating, ideally incorporating the first dopamine release early in the narrative. Some examples are provided below:

- *"Last year I traveled to Hong Kong to attend a sustainability conference at the HKCEC (Hong Kong Convention and Exhibition Centre). When I left my home in London on that late September afternoon, I could barely have imagined that it was going to be one of the most complicated journeys of my entire life. . ."*

- *"The design team had worked hard on the new prototype and was relieved to meet the Friday deadline. But when they handed it over, they could never have anticipated their client's reaction. . ."*

- *"There are several common reasons for this. Some which you might easily imagine, but others that you would certainly not expect. . ."*

Each of these statements acts as a dopamine trigger. The minds of your audience will be activated, visualizing the situation faced by the characters, trying to fill in the gaps, and imagining different scenarios. What will happen next and how will the story continue?

Think about how you pace your story to build up to an event, bringing the audience with you. Induce curiosity and an element of suspense through an interesting question, a suspenseful statement, or by sharing an unexpected twist.

One of the simplest ways to trigger a dopamine release in verbal narration is through the timely insertion of a pause at a critical point in the narrative. Pause before you tell them what happened. Don't rush.

"The doctor glanced through the test results, stared blankly into space with a half-confused expression and said . . . [pause]. . . "This is miraculous!""

Dopamine triggers, when used periodically, act as an effective engagement mechanism. At the same time, don't over-use them. You can't keep people on the edge of their chairs all the time!

Oxytocin

Oxytocin, one of the brain's most powerful neurochemicals, is released when we feel empathy: our ability to experience others' emotions. It appeals to our humanity, warming the heart, increasing our feeling of trust, generosity, and social bonding.

Its release is experienced by many when petting an animal, playing with a happy young child, or even watching dog videos. If you are moved when watching a film or feel a tear in your eye, that's the sign of an oxytocin release.

Oxytocin can be used in storytelling to build a relationship, either with the narrator or a character (or characters) in a story. As a result, we lower our guard, become more open to listen, and more willing to cooperate.

Oxytocin triggers are often used in charity campaigns. Scenes of starving children in developing countries make us feel more humane and willing to make donations. They can also act as an emotional ambition changer. After watching a superhero movie, you might feel bonding with the main character, inclined to mimic their behavior, feeling powerful and ready to save the world.[4]

A company selling elevator systems had been pitching to the landlords of an old building in the center of Paris, France. The six-floor residential building in a quiet corner of the city had an antiquated elevator dating back to the early 1900s.

The elevator broke down frequently and required regular service visits. Parts were increasingly difficult to obtain. The loud noise of the motor disturbed residents on the upper floors and its energy consumption elevated the building's monthly costs.

Presentations including impressive facts and figures had been made, boasting the benefits of installing a new, up-to-date system, but the bottom line was that the landlords simply didn't want to spend the money. Determined to overcome this, the sales manager decided to take a different approach and talk to some of the residents in the building. At the next meeting with the landlords, he opened with a story.

There was a man living on the top floor of the building who was old, frail, and bound to a wheelchair. His wheelchair would not fit into the elevator, so twice each week his son would come and visit. He would carry his father down the six flights of stairs, they would sit in the park and drink coffee, and then he would carry his father up again.

The landlords were horrified about the impact of the issue on their residents, and in the same meeting requested a proposal for its replacement.

Honesty in your stories and a willingness to paint a less-than-perfect picture of the world can be a major factor in triggering the release of oxytocin. These triggers do not have to revolve around tragic stories but usually concern a struggle, perhaps a story based on your own experience that others will recognize.

Use of such examples shows the audience that you are just like them, increasing their bond with you and their willingness to listen. A senior project manager addressing 300 colleagues at a conference in Dallas, USA, used this technique in the opening of her talk:

> *"Sometimes people ask me about the most challenging project that I have ever experienced. Mine took place in Montreal, Canada, in the Spring of 2010. We were behind schedule. The client was unhappy and had been mismanaged. A volcanic eruption in Iceland had prevented us from flying in some of our strongest team members. And a critical deadline was approaching. But we managed, and today I'd like to talk about what we did to turn the situation around . . ."*

By talking about your own failures or struggles, you make an emotional connection with your audience. You become accessible and relatable. Humans don't like to get their fingers burned, but when we do, it presents one of the greatest and immediate sources of learning. That's why the sharing of practical lessons is so powerful in storytelling. The challenges faced and the recovery strategies that succeeded capture our attention.

Oxytocin can also be triggered by building empathy around one of the main characters in your story.

> *"This was not only Merrick's first job after graduating, but also his first visit to New York City. As he slowly ascended to the 37th floor in the glass elevator just off Wall Street, he felt a knot in his stomach. He straightened his collar and tie, cleared his throat and braced himself to enter a new world as the elevator doors slowly opened . . ."*

Don't underestimate the impact of empathy in the stories that we build in business. Describing a situation faced by either yourself, a colleague, or client may be the spark needed to motivate action.

Endorphin

Endorphin is the "feel good" chemical. It's released primarily when we smile, laugh, or find something amusing. It makes people focused and attentive, yet at the same time creative and relaxed.

The release of endorphin warms up your audience, creating rapport and likeability, enhancing your relationship with them. It makes you a more interesting person to listen to. Endorphin can easily be triggered using dry humor. Try to introduce it early in your session, even as part of your introduction.

> *"As you can probably tell from my gray hair, I've worked as an account manager for over 20 years . . ."*

At the start of her commencement speech for Harvard University, J.K. Rowling, the author of the famous Harry Potter fiction book series, alluded to the natural fear of giving a speech on a big stage, and her very human reaction to it.

> *"The first thing I would like to say is 'thank you'. Not only has Harvard given me an extraordinary honor, but the weeks of fear and nausea I have endured at the thought of giving this commencement address have actually made me lose weight! A win-win situation. Now all I have to do is take deep breaths, squint at the red banners, and convince myself that I am at the world's largest Gryffindor reunion."*

Endorphin increases engagement. People certainly won't be disengaged when they are laughing. Decide when to embed elements of humor into your narrative. You might talk about a happy moment that will resonate with others, tell a story about something that went catastrophically wrong but that is funny in hindsight, share a humorous anecdote, talk about the strange and unexpected behavior of a character, or share an exaggerated emotion.

> *"When we received the long-awaited report, it looked like it had been written by a monkey! It was badly structured and showed little reflection of the real issue at hand."*

At the same time, remember that in business your primary purpose is not to entertain. The use of subtle dry humor tends to be most effective. Ensure that your anecdotes tie back to your main message and are effective in illustrating your point.

Cortisol

Cortisol is our primary stress hormone, produced when something warrants our attention. It's like a response to a distress signal or warning sign. If we perceive a potential threat or hear something distressing in a story, if we feel afraid or startled, cortisol is the flashing red light that commands our undivided attention.

Cortisol can be beneficial in storytelling when used in small doses. As humans, we crave adventure and a sense of risk, which is why many of us enjoy reading thrillers and crime novels. Small releases of cortisol capture the attention of your audience, helping them focus and putting them in a better position to connect and resonate with your content.

In business, we usually use cortisol in the narrative to create urgency:

- *"Failure to succeed in this project could have a disastrous impact on our organization. We could all lose our jobs!"*
- *"We'll give you one last chance to solve the problem. Otherwise, the contract will be terminated."*
- *"The next 3 months are the most critical. If we can make it through them, we will be on the home stretch."*

Beware of releasing too much cortisol. This causes an unpleasant and disturbing feeling, making your audience uncomfortable, critical, and inclined to raise their guard. When someone switches the TV channel, feeling disturbed after the first 30 minutes of a horror movie, the reason is probably an excess of cortisol. They stop watching and try to forget the experience as quickly as possible.

Adrenaline

Adrenaline, commonly known as the "fight or flight" hormone, is produced by the adrenal glands just above the kidneys. It is released, often in conjunction with cortisol, after receiving a message from the brain that a stressful situation has occurred but at the same time creates a feeling of excitement.

When you watch an action movie, it's the reason that your heart begins to race as if you were one of the characters on the screen. Your muscles tense, you breathe faster, and you may even break a light sweat. Along with the increase in heart rate, adrenaline focuses your attention and gives you the same surge of energy that you would need to run away from a dangerous situation.

In business we can release adrenaline by talking about stressful situations that resonate with the audience or by narrating the rapid progress of events:

- *"You know that feeling when you have just three hours to meet a deadline?"*

- *"The client demanded an answer within 10 minutes as their management meeting was about to begin. Nathan was at a loss. None of his team members knew what to say. He tried calling his project manager but couldn't reach him. Then his director, but she was on a plane to Beijing. There seemed little chance of finding a solution in time. Meanwhile, the client was pacing in the hallway outside his office, becoming increasingly agitated . . ."*

Use neurochemical releases wisely in the narrative

Triggering neurochemical releases should be a conscious decision when designing the narrative, particularly when selecting the examples and anecdotes to be included. Which ones will trigger dopamine, oxytocin, or endorphin? And will you trigger cortisol and adrenaline at all or avoid them?

- Dopamine triggers are powerful in creating interest through suspense and the quest to know a resolution or outcome.

- Oxytocin triggers are an essential factor when empathy, generosity, and supportive behaviors are required.

- Endorphin can be used to warm your audience, create likeability, and maintain engagement.

- Adrenaline and cortisol should be used more selectively. Their over-use can make an audience feel uncomfortable, critical, and inclined to tune-out.

Emotional triggers play an important role in stories

Having introduced the role of neurochemicals we can discuss the use of emotional triggers in a story, which typically involves a combination of neurochemicals.

Stories in business are designed to drive some form of action. But humans are not usually willing to act unless they have been emotionally aroused. Consider the following example.

One Saturday, you go to a large shopping mall. You see an old lady who, while balancing her shopping bags, drops her walking stick. You walk over, pick it up, and hand it back to her. You did a good deed and helped her out.

This example revolves around an emotional trigger, one of *empathy*. You acted because you were emotionally evoked by the event that you saw. The same principle applies to the stories that we tell in business.

A consulting team addressing a technology organization in Portugal began their narrative with the words:

"The market is changing rapidly, putting you under tremendous pressure. You will need to act quickly to retain your leading position . . ."

These words were designed to evoke the emotion of *urgency*. They wanted executives to lean forward in their chairs and think "This is important. We'd better give this our full attention." This was embedded into the narrative by design, not by accident.

This principle can work equally well when addressing audiences within your own organization:

A senior manager in India had recently taken over responsibility for an organization of 300 people. She was planning to speak at her first all-employee meeting.

Her initial intention was to open with the statement, "*We need change!*," which was exactly what management had appointed her to drive. But what perception would this have created among her employees? Probably not a positive one. "A new boss. Now everything has to change? Great!" Giving this some further reflection she reframed her message:

"This organization has achieved many good things, but now we have the opportunity to move ourselves up the value chain. And these are the things that we will need to do to achieve that. . ."

Her words were designed to evoke the emotion of motivation. To mobilize her organization and encourage people to see new potential.

Emotional triggers can be used to evoke a wide range of emotions: happiness, inspiration, pride, relief, urgency, concern, and frustration, to name just a few. When you raise an important point in a story, you want an emotional reaction from your audience. Which one is it?

Designing a compelling narrative requires you to first identify the emotional responses that you need from your audience to get the job done. How do you want people to feel? Then build in the right triggers to evoke them.

Part 4: Descriptive detail and the role of characters in a story

Descriptive detail is used in storytelling to provide your audience with an experience. Personalization is used to increase the resonance of your ideas. And the inclusion of characters makes the story more relatable and memorable.

Descriptive detail activates the visualization engine

Descriptive detail has an important role to play in activating the visualization engine in the minds of your audience. You don't just want people to hear the story, you want them to experience it. This is what drives your key points home and makes them memorable. James Bond likes his martinis shaken not stirred. Abstract ideas don't stick. Detailed ones do.

There will be times when you need a concise story that is sharp, to the point, made of clear assertions with intact logical relationships that lead quickly to a conclusion. At the same time, stories that are too concise lack the build-up and detail required to be visualized impactfully. Apply this idea with moderation. Long, verbose, over-complicated sentences should certainly be avoided. They become boring, go off on tangents, and include irrelevant detail. People's eyes glaze over and their thoughts wander. "Get to the point!," they think, "Where is this going?" Achieve a good balance by sticking to the key points in your story blueprint but making sure that you elaborate them well.

When you *describe something in detail* the occipital and temporal lobes of your brain light up as your senses and emotions are engaged, as if you can actually see and hear the scene. Research shows that the listener's brain activity follows that of the speaker with a slight delay, a phenomenon known as *neural coupling*.[5] This is how we turn a story into an experience for the audience. Compare the following statements and consider which one is easier to visualize:

- *"From the beginning of the meeting the CFO seemed skeptical."*
- *"From the beginning of the meeting the CFO, a grim-looking character with graying hair and an unruly beard, seemed skeptical."*

Details also help us to validate a story's truthfulness. The mind doesn't handle abstractions well. The more evidence we have in the form of specific and concrete details, the more likely we are to believe in it.

Use a descriptive starting point to set the scene

Take the time to describe the situation clearly so that the audience can visualize it.

"I was walking out of the National Convention Center in Shanghai, China, on a bright Spring afternoon where I had been attending a conference

on diversity, equity, and inclusion. Two gentlemen were walking ahead of me. One, a bearded, professor-like figure in gray flannel pants, moccasins, and a tweed jacket. The other, somewhat younger, casually dressed, carrying a rucksack on his shoulder. They were talking about differences in culture and sharing strongly conflicting opinions . . ."

Appeal to the five senses when describing a situation

Descriptive detail often leverages the five senses. Explain how it felt, looked, tasted, sounded, or smelled when narrating an example. This will help the listener to connect and experience:

- *"The crashing sound of his typing was driving me mad."*
- *"An aroma of fresh coffee filled the café."*
- *"We could taste deception in the air."*
- *"She felt a lump in her throat."*
- *"A chill went down his spine."*

Emphatic vocabulary can be used to increase momentum

Don't be afraid to use bold vocabulary to create emphasis within your narrative. You're not likely to inspire people using dull words.

If something is a fantastic idea, then say that it's a *fantastic* idea. You might equally tell your audience that *"delaying a project could have catastrophic effects."* These are big words but, if used appropriately, add momentum to your messaging.

Personalization brings your message home

A narrative that is personal and specific has greater impact than one that is generic or abstract. There are three ways to achieve this:

1. **Use of possessive adjectives:** Don't talk to your client about "the launch plan" but instead *"your* launch plan." It's more personal and resonates better. Don't talk about the status of the project, talk about the status of *our* project. Make it more collaborative. These small changes increase the resonance of your messaging.

2. **Put a human face on it:** Another powerful personalization technique is to put a human face on an idea. Ideas are often discussed at an abstract level, yet abstraction is your enemy in storytelling.

   Instead of talking about "the lack of internet coverage in rural America," talk about why "Emily, a young girl in Arizona, can't do home schooling due to the lack of broadband availability in her area."

   And instead of talking about "the failing healthcare system," explain why "Jack, a pensioner in Ohio, keeps having difficulty getting his prescriptions fulfilled."

3. **Scale back the numbers:** Problems of scale also constitute a form of abstraction. Hearing about 100,000 COVID deaths is tragic but doesn't move us. The magnitude is difficult to relate to. Hearing about

one death, the circumstances, and the impact on the family does. Once you have evoked emotion, you can then link it to the greater cause.

Characters can play an important role in stories

A good way to introduce descriptive detail in a story is to include characters that the audience can imagine, empathize with, and, in the case of longer stories, build relationships with. Three considerations are particularly important when introducing characters:

1. **Take the time to introduce the characters in your story:** Give them names where possible. Sometimes these names may need to be fictitious in lieu of confidentiality, but it still makes the characters more relatable. Many of the examples in this book use this technique. In Chapter 2, you met Chloe, a design architect, and her manager, Adam, who were preparing a presentation for a client. These characters make the examples more real and memorable.

2. **You may sometimes be the main character in your own story:** This is quite acceptable and makes your job even easier. You are simply relating an experience, explaining the challenges that you faced, how you felt, and the problems that you had to overcome. You are telling it the way you remember it.

3. **Use the active voice rather than the summarizing voice:** If there are characters in your story, dialogue between them becomes important. Try to use the active voice, citing their exact words which are real events, rather than the summarizing voice that

quotes "he said" or "she said," which is much less engaging. Observe the use of the active voice in the example below.

Keisha, a senior consultant, was delivering a project for a large pharmaceutical company in Africa. Her team reported to Nomonde, a director in the client organization, a woman with high standards and a reputation for good performance in all the projects that she supervised.

From the inception of the project the team noticed that Nomonde always seemed to be stressed. She would call them once or twice a day. *"What is the status of this task?,"* she would ask, *"And what is the progress on this issue?"* The team was always able to reassure her. Everything was on track as detailed in the weekly reports. But day after day the phone calls continued.

Keisha eventually raised this point with her team. *"This is not the type of relationship we aim to have with our clients,"* she said, *"Perhaps we should reconsider the way we communicate?"*

They realized that Nomonde was responsible for several projects and several different teams. She probably spent a good part of each day calling different project managers with similar questions to ensure that there would be no slippage.

"Let's take a proactive step and adjust our communication approach," one of the team members suggested. *"We could send Nomonde a brief informal*

status report at the end of each day." The daily emails that they began sending summarized tasks completed that day, tasks planned for the next, and the status of any ongoing issues.

The change in client behavior that resulted was quite remarkable. Not only did the questions stop coming, but at weekly meetings Nomonde would say, *"I like this team. You are the ones that I don't have to worry about."*

Part 5: Interaction and navigation can be essential in achieving your intended outcome

Storytelling in business is not usually a one-way dialogue. Presenting for 20 minutes in the boardroom gives little guarantee that the audience will simply adopt your recommendations. Some form of interaction will be required to ensure that your points have been understood, reinforced where needed, and that concerns have been addressed.

Achieving your vision is a process of delivering information that is closely coupled with logic, while seeking input and validation. Building interaction into your story ensures that you have the dialogue that you need with your audience.

When delivering a story, you can interact with your audience any time you like, but always plan your key interactions in advance.

The cornerstones of an interaction approach can be planned in advance

In our example in Chapter 1, Dan, a program manager, was flying to Germany to deliver a presentation concerning a project planning and control methodology to a team of client executives. His vision was:

> *To gain our client's confidence in the use of our planning and control approach in technology projects and to address any associated concerns*

Figure 5.3 illustrates the delivery plan that he had created for this presentation.

Dan had designed a presentation of 10 slides to be delivered over a 45-minute timeline, allowing time for client input and questions.

- He would begin with opening words, emphasizing the importance of the session, followed by presenter and topic introductions.
- An agenda would illustrate the intended structure of the session.
- The main body of the presentation, the story, was divided into four sections.
- At the end, a summary would bring a new twist on the content presented, leveraging lessons learned from similar engagements.

The audience interaction approach that he had planned in advance is shown on the right of Figure 5.3.

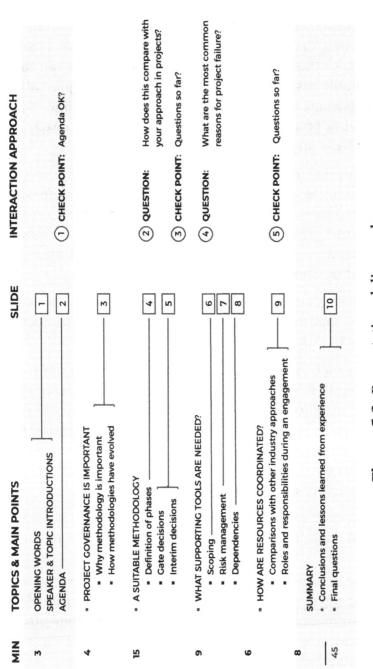

Figure 5.3: Presentation delivery plan

- **Interaction 1:** A check point after presenting the agenda. *"Is this agenda OK with you?"* Some hesitate to take this check point in case they receive an unfavorable response, but if there is any misalignment, it's important that you know as early as possible, maximizing your opportunity to adapt your approach and address any discrepancies.

- **Interaction 2:** Having provided an initial introduction to the methodology, he would ask: *"How does this compare with the way that you manage your projects today?"* The intention was to engage the audience, have a conversation and better understand their current position.

- **Interaction 3:** Another check point having discussed the methodology to catch any questions before moving on.

- **Interaction 4:** Here he planned to flip his approach around. Before opening the next topic, he would ask the question, *"In your experience, what are the most common reasons for projects to fail?,"* suspecting that some of the responses would relate to scoping, risk management and dependencies. This would set the stage very nicely for the material that followed.

- **Interaction 5:** A final check point to answer any remaining questions before beginning the summary.

These interactions were designed to trigger the dialogue needed to achieve his vision. They would help him to manage a natural dialogue, gain further inputs, address concerns, and ultimately gain the acceptance of his audience.

Interaction is possible in many forms

A variety of interaction techniques can be used during the delivery of a story. A selection of the most common is provided below.

Techniques suitable for most audiences:

- **Check points** represent the simplest type of inter-action. They can be used regularly, are the least time-consuming form of interaction, but require the audience to do the least amount of work. Participants may simply nod without getting involved in the dialogue.

- **Open questions** are more likely to start a conversation and are good for soliciting input. If nobody responds to the question and the room falls silent, be ready to recover and respond, yourself, with a comment.

- **Directing questions to specific individuals** can be powerful, particularly if members of the audience are knowledgeable and willing to share their experience. But be careful not to put people on the spot. If you direct a question to an individual, be sure that they would be comfortable to answer. If in doubt, and if you know the individual, ask their permission in advance.

Techniques suited to larger audiences:

- **Polls** work well with audiences, both large and small. *"Can we have a show of hands? How many people have experienced this issue?"* As the hands go up, the response is non-verbal, but yet you are still engaging your audience.

- **Focus group exercises** work well in workshop situations. Put a question forward to the participants and say, *"Get together with the four or five people sitting closest to you. Spend five minutes discussing how you would answer this question. Then we'll collect a few answers from the audience and see what you think . . ."*

- **The "you question"** enables you to simulate a dialogue. A useful technique when dealing with a large audience or recording a video where a two-way dialogue may be difficult or impossible. Describe a situation and then inject a "you question," such as *"How would you react in a situation like that?"* Pause for a few seconds before you continue. Your audience will use the pause to try and answer the "you question" in their minds. "How would I react in that situation?" You are drawing them into your material and getting them to participate, even in the absence of a two-way dialogue.

A mix of these interaction techniques is generally most effective. Audiences rarely respond well to monologue. An interactive approach is more engaging, also making the speaker's job easier. It creates a more relaxed and natural environment. The timing of your interactions is also important.

Make your first interaction early, usually within the first 2–3 minutes of your delivery.

By doing this, you are giving your audience a signal that this will be an interactive session. They will prepare themselves, mentally, to interact with you. Don't wait for

10 minutes before making your first interaction. By then people will have become comfortable in their chairs and switched into listening-mode. A cold audience will be more difficult to engage.

In some cases, an alternative navigation approach may be required

Navigation refers to the order in which you present your content. The flow of your story has already been designed in your story blueprint, but you may need to adapt this on the fly to address unexpected needs and priorities. This requires some flexibility! You may present a well-formulated agenda, but what if your audience is impatient and wants to skip ahead?

This is exactly what happened to Dan, our program manager, delivering his presentation about methodology. He presented his agenda, took a check point, and received the following response from the client executives:

> *"We are already familiar enough with methodologies! We can skip that part. What interests us today are supporting tools and the management of resources."*

Such reactions are not uncommon. Your audience may have particular issues front-of-mind and be unwilling to wait until you reach that part of your story.

When a story has a deductive flow, each part of the story somehow relies on those that preceded it. Dan needed to make a careful decision, and responded:

"That's understood. If you'd bear with me for just a few minutes, I'd like to show you some aspects of this methodology that have an important impact on tools and resources. Once we've done that, I'll be happy to move on the areas that interest you and we can spend the majority of our time discussing them."

This enabled him to maintain the logical flow of the story but also to satisfy the appetite of the audience. Apply good judgment regarding points that need to be mentioned before skipping ahead, even if they are covered verbally, without the use of supporting presentation material. A good storyteller balances good preparation with flexibility!

Chapter summary

- A typical delivery is divided into five phases, each of which requires careful planning:

  -Opening words

  -Speaker introduction

  -Topic introduction

  -Main body

  -Closing words.

- The narrative is where you tell your story. Consider the use of:

  -Metaphors, analogies, and anecdotes to improve the way that your key points are visualized.

  -Emotional triggers to influence the feelings and reactions of your audience, to gain their support or inspire action.

  -Descriptive detail enabling your audience to visualize and experience the story.

  -Personalization to increase resonance of ideas.

  -The use of characters to make your examples more relatable.

- Storytelling is usually a two-way dialogue. Plan your key audience interactions in advance.

- Alternative navigation approaches may be needed to address changing audience priorities.

Next steps

The ideas presented in this chapter can only be mastered through practice. Consider the next story that you plan to present:

- How will you approach each of the five presentation phases?

- Try to use each of the following linguistic constructs at least once: metaphor, analogy, anecdote.

- Plan the use of descriptive detail during at least one part of your story.

- Plan the use of neurochemical releases, as appropriate to your topic.

- Define your key audience interactions in advance.

Notes

1. Lara Boyd, "After watching this, your brain will not be the same." TEDx, Vancouver, 2015.
2. *New York Times*, "How Prince Philip navigated the most challenging of corporate dress codes." October 4, 2021.
3. Ric Elias, "3 things I learned while my plane crashed." TED Talk, Long Beach, CA, 2011.
4. Paul J. Zak, "Why your brain loves good storytelling." *HBR*, October 28, 2014.
5. Greg J. Stephens, Lauren J. Silbert, and Joseph Hasson, "Speaker-listener neural coupling underlies successful communication." *Proceedings of National Academy of Science, U.S.A.*, 107(32) (2010): 14425–14430.

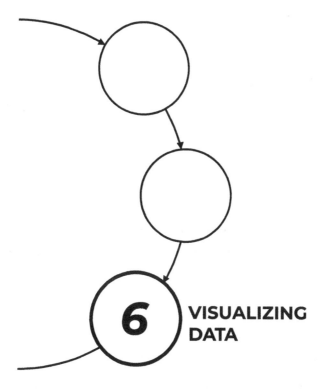

6 VISUALIZING DATA

Data plays an important role in many stories, but only when it communicates a clear message through effective visualization

CHAPTER SIX

VISUALIZING DATA

In many business domains, such as finance, technology and numerous others, data can play an important role in telling a story. Most data sets contain several different messages. It's important to identify and communicate the right one. Ask yourself, what does this data say? What story does it tell? And how should I communicate it to my audience?

When you present a chart, you shouldn't need to explain it for five minutes before people understand the story that it tells. The audience should be able to look at the chart and decode the key messages, themselves, within 7–10 seconds.

Data visualization is about communicating a message quickly, clearly, and effortlessly.

This chapter will provide a short introduction to the extensive science of data visualization, sharing ideas that can be applied immediately to data-driven stories. We will start by exploring the psychological character-istics of the visualization system, discuss the use of the most common chart types, and finally share some prac-tical formatting tips that will increase the impact of the data that you present.

The visualization system hinges on three types of memory

We are all equipped with a visualization system that gov-erns the way we interpret data. It's based on three types of memory: the iconic memory, the working memory, and the long-term memory (Figure 6.1). Learning how this system works is the key to unleashing the power of data visualization.

The iconic memory is fast-moving, but instantaneous

The iconic memory is fast-moving. It processes hundreds of events every minute. But most of what it processes it simply discards.

Figure 6.1: Three types of memory

When driving to work yesterday you might have spotted a white BMW SUV that cut in front of you just before your exit. But you didn't think about it for more than half a second because nothing bad happened. That information was simply discarded.

A few minutes earlier as you drove along the highway you might have seen a bill-board advertisement for pizza on the roadside, but you probably didn't feel like eating pizza at eight o'clock in the morning. Once again, the information was processed, but immediately discarded.

This is how the iconic memory continues to work until it spots something that it finds interesting or relevant. It then grabs that information and passes it on to the second type of memory: the working memory.

The working memory is where all the work is done

Consider the working memory as your analysis engine. Some debate whether "short-term" memory and "working" memory are the same thing. The difference is that the short-term memory holds information for a limited amount of time, whereas the working memory also tries to manipulate the information and draw conclusions.

Research has indicated that people can only process about four chunks of visual information in their working memory at any given time. Put in more than that, which is easily done when you are working with data, and it becomes overloaded.

Overloading the working memory is like throwing glue into a machine. Its performance downgrades significantly and, as a result, it's unlikely to compute a useful result. If we can avoid overloading the working memory and a useful result is computed, the result will be passed on to the third type of memory: the long-term memory.

The long-term memory is where decisions are made, and where commitment is secured

The long-term memory is our intended destination. If you are successful in reaching it, your message has been fully understood and absorbed by your audience. This gives them the confidence to act and take decisions. People don't like to act on things that they don't fully understand.

Memory has an important impact on data visualization

Having understood the three types of memory, consider how their relationships apply to the principles of data visualization.

> **In data visualization the aim is to appeal to the iconic memory, to avoid overloading the working memory, and to ensure that the intended message reaches the long-term memory**

Achieving this requires some careful consideration in the way that you represent your data. Overloading the working memory is easily done. Take a look at the example in Figure 6.2. If this was presented to you, how would you interpret it?

If you have strong analytical skills you might start to look for high numbers, low numbers, and trends, however,

MONTHLY SALES HAVE SHOWN VARYING PERFORMANCE

	Jan	Feb	Mar	Apr	May	Jun	Jul	Aug	Sep	Oct	Nov	Dec
Central	$42.759	$47.743	$51.075	$49.825	$54.010	$61.321	$68.250	$70.038	$76.328	$82.075	$83.475	$95.385
East	$43.000	$42.850	$41.995	$45.850	$43.372	$36.328	$32.385	$37.342	$46.950	$50.375	$46.251	$39.100
South	$75.500	$73.650	$72.980	$72.980	$71.438	$69.500	$71.150	$66.359	$69.352	$64.287	$66.247	$65.295
West	$15.272	$15.735	$16.500	$19.520	$20.980	$21.795	$23.594	$22.759	$25.243	$27.500	$29.513	$28.955

Figure 6.2: Data displayed in matrix format

most people wouldn't exercise that much brain power. The working memory has been overloaded, and as a result we read no clear message as the basis for action.

If we apply the principles of data visualization to the same data set, we might represent it using the multi-line chart, illustrated in Figure 6.3. Here you can quickly see that region Central had the highest sales at year end, whereas region South used to have the highest sales. You can see that region East has a seasonal performance with a drop in the summer, whereas region West has been growing slowly but organically. You would decode these messages easily within seven to ten seconds, *quickly*, *clearly*, and *effortlessly*.

Select the right type of chart for the right message

Charts help people to understand complicated data sets, find patterns, make comparisons, and observe trends. The sections below provide examples of some of the most common chart types, and the messages that they best illustrate.

> **Selecting an optimal chart format helps the working memory, by making the intended message as easy as possible to decode.**

Big number charts "hero" the number

Big number charts place the most emphasis on a number, with any annotations around it coming in second place (Figure 6.4).

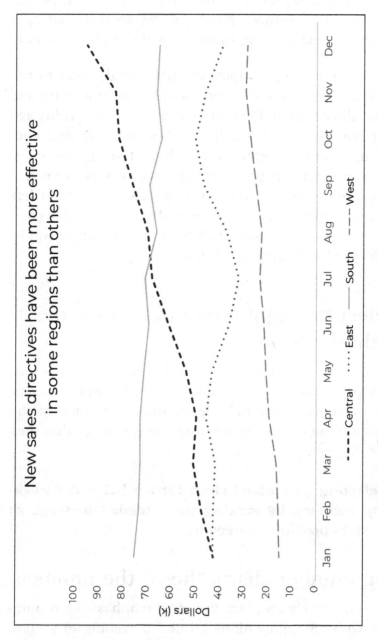

Figure 6.3: Data visualized using a multi-line chart

PARIS AÉROPORT

57,461,426
PASSENGERS 2022

Figure 6.4: Big number representation

Big number charts work well in situations where the number itself does the talking. The reader will see it and understand the message immediately.

A point of caution with this type of chart is that the number must be presented in a context relevant to the audience. In the example above, do the readers know if 57 million passengers is a good or bad number for the airport in Paris, France?

As we saw earlier in Jensen's presentation slides for SmartStream, a set of big numbers can be used that collectively support a message (Figure 6.5).

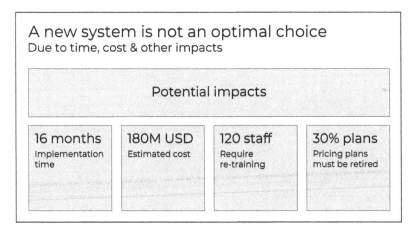

Figure 6.5: A set of big numbers supporting a message

Comparison charts allow visual comparison between one or more data sets

Comparison charts, such as line charts, column charts, bar charts, and cluster charts guide the reader in the comparison of one or more data sets or indicate differences over time.

The line chart

The line chart (Figure 6.6) is used to show the trend of a continuous category or its performance over time.

Consider the example in Figure 6.6. When you read this chart, the message that you are likely to decode is that "sales were increasing nicely at the beginning of the year. They plateaued for a while, and now they have been increasing again as year-end approaches."

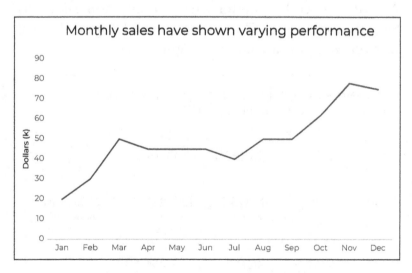

Figure 6.6: Simple line chart

Figure 6.7: Line + big number representation

Now look at Figure 6.7 where we combine the line chart and big number chart formats.

The message that you read from the chart will now be different. Your first impression is likely to be "Look, November sales are up at 78,000 dollars." Nothing in the data has changed, but you decoded a different message. We have simply moved your iconic memory to where we want it to be to control your interpretation of the data. This involves the use of a *pre-attentive attribute*, which we will discuss later in the chapter.

The multi-line chart, shown earlier in Figure 6.3, is effective in comparing the performance of multiple categories. Try to avoid exceeding seven categories when using this type of chart to avoid overcrowding. If two categories of different measure are being compared, different Y-axes may also be used, illustrated in Figure 6.8.

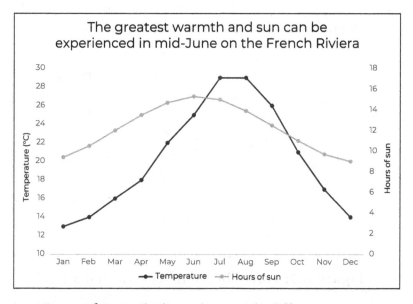

Figure 6.8: Multi-line chart with different Y-axes

Bar and column charts

Bar and column charts are used primarily for comparison. These formats can be used interchangeably to some degree; however:

- **Column charts** are preferable in situations that involve chronology, for example, when presenting data over the months of the year. They are also effective when your data contains negative values. A downward direction on a vertical access naturally signals negation.

- **Bar charts** are better in situations where more than nine categories are displayed, as column charts easily become cluttered. They are also useful in situations where long category labels are needed, not easily accommodated on a column chart.

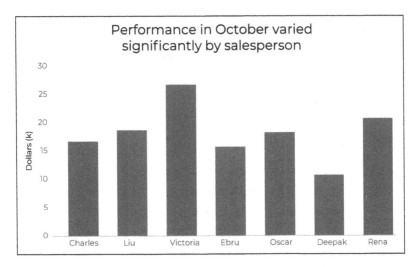

Figure 6.9: Column chart example

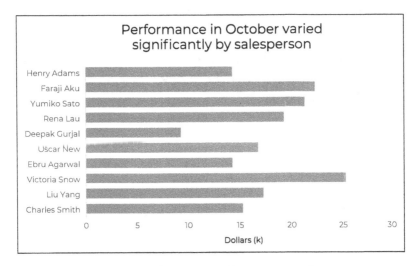

Figure 6.10: Bar chart example

Relationship charts illustrate connections and correlations

Relationship charts, such as scatter plots, illustrate connections and correlations.

The scatterplot

The scatterplot shows the relationship between two variables (Figure 6.11). Data points are shown on the chart, with the horizontal axis representing one variable and the vertical axis representing the other. Scatterplots are useful for showing patterns and trends in data, as well as for identifying outliers.

Distribution charts draw attention to trends and outliers

Charts, such as histograms (Figure 6.12), show how data points are distributed by frequency, drawing attention to trends and outliers.

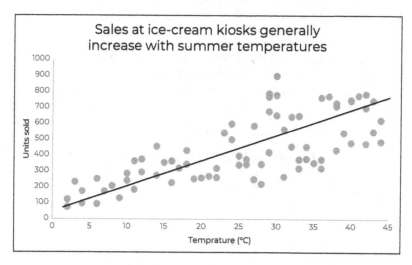

Figure 6.11: Scatterplot representation

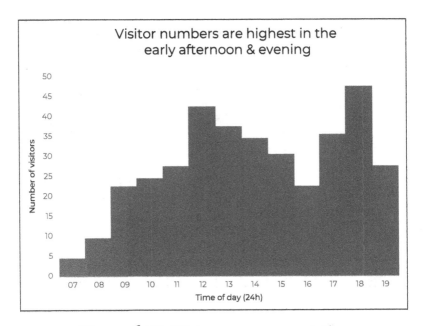

Figure 6.12: Histogram representation

Composition charts show the parts of a whole

Composition charts, such as stacked column charts, stacked area charts, and pie charts, show the parts of a whole.

The stacked column chart

Stacked column charts are used to show the sum of parts to a whole as well as the trend in totals (Figure 6.13).

Compare the use of a stacked column chart in Figure 6.13 with the use of a cluster chart, an evolution of the column chart in Figure 6.14, representing the same data set. Which chart do you prefer?

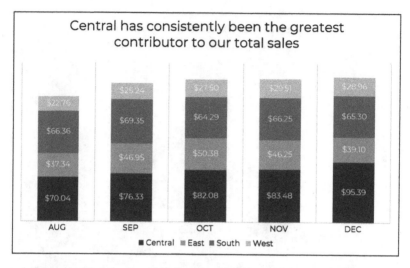

Figure 6.13: Stacked column chart representation

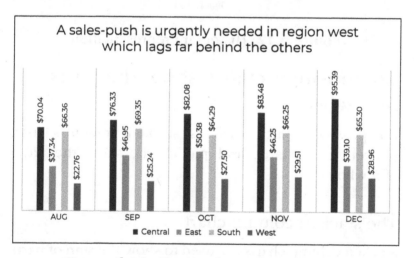

Figure 6.14: Cluster chart representation

The answer is that both are good charts but communicate two different messages. If your story is about the sum of parts to a whole and the trend in totals, the stacked column chart, a composition chart, is the one to use. If you want to emphasize differences in performance, the cluster chart, a comparison chart, is the one to use. Pick the right chart to communicate the right message!

The stacked area chart

The stacked area chart is a composite chart useful for showing the sum of parts to a whole over a linear axis, such as time (Figure 6.15).

The pie chart

The popular pie chart divides a circular area into sectors that describe numerical proportions that add to a total of 100%, comparing the sum of parts of a whole. Use it to compare just a few categories in a way that makes your message clear.

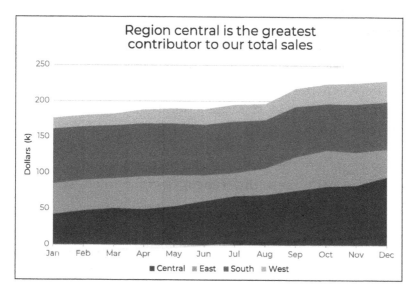

Figure 6.15: Stacked area representation

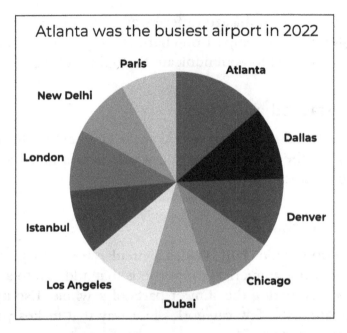

Figure 6.16: Busiest airports 2022

As soon as the segments in a pie chart become similar in size, it becomes difficult to read, which is why many avoid it. Figure 6.16 shows the distribution of traffic between the busiest airports in 2022. Is the Dallas segment greater in size than the Denver segment? It's difficult to tell.

If we represent the same dataset with a bar chart, shown in Figure 6.17, these differences become much clearer.

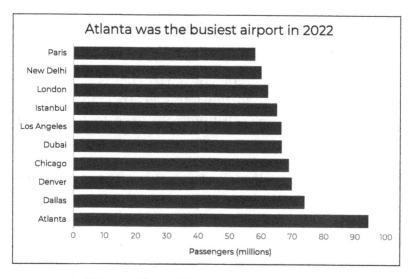

Figure 6.17: Busiest airports 2022

An evolution of the pie chart is the ring chart, where the center space can also be used effectively to include a big number (Figure 6.18).

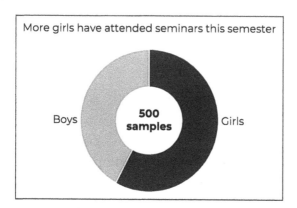

Figure 6.18: Ring chart representation

Pre-attentive attributes accelerate audience interpretation

Selecting the right type of chart helps the working memory to decode the intended message quickly, whereas pre-attentive attributes are used to trigger the iconic memory.

> **Pre-attentive attributes draw the attention of the iconic memory to what the author wants to be seen as most important, creating a visual hierarchy of information.**

Largely driven by formatting, such as size, color, the thickness of a line and position, they trigger the iconic memory to process information very quickly without us even realizing it. This is the reason why certain visual elements can grab our attention so easily. Take a look at the example in Figure 6.19. How many number "5's" do you see?

```
6 8 7 7 3 3 0 3 5 0 3 9 3 3 0 5 0 0 0 2 0 3 0 3
3 4 4 9 2 2 0 0 4 0 4 0 0 7 0 6 6 0 0 0 0 5 7
4 9 3 5 3 0 0 3 3 0 3 0 0 2 0 2 0 0 2 0 1 0 0 1 7
2 3 3 9 8 4 8 2 8 3 9 0 4 0 9 0 9 8 8 2 9 0 4 8 2
2 3 4 8 9 0 2 3 5 4 8 3 9 0 8 4 9 0 8 9 8 5 0 1 0
0 2 0 0 0 7 2 0 2 1 1 1 1 2 8 3 5 7 4 8 0 9 0 2
0 2 4 9 0 2 9 3 9 7 2 0 3 3 6 8 7 2 0 1 9 7 0 0 1
```

Figure 6.19: Sample data set

The addition of highlights, shown in Figure 6.20, would have made that task much easier. Use them to draw the iconic memory to where it needs to be to locate the intended message or answer.

6	8	7	7	3	3	0	3	**5**	0	3	9	3	3	0	**5**	0	0	0	0	2	0	3	0	3
3	4	4	9	2	2	0	0	4	0	4	0	0	7	0	6	6	0	0	0	0	0	0	**5**	7
4	9	3	**5**	3	0	0	3	3	0	3	0	0	2	0	2	0	0	2	0	1	0	0	1	7
2	3	3	9	8	4	8	2	8	3	9	0	4	0	9	0	9	8	8	2	9	0	4	8	2
2	3	4	8	9	0	2	3	**5**	4	8	3	9	0	8	4	9	0	8	9	8	**5**	0	1	0
0	2	0	0	0	7	2	0	2	1	1	1	1	2	8	3	**5**	7	4	8	0	9	0	2	
0	2	4	9	0	2	9	3	9	7	2	0	3	3	6	8	7	2	0	1	9	7	0	0	1

Figure 6.20: Sample data set with highlights

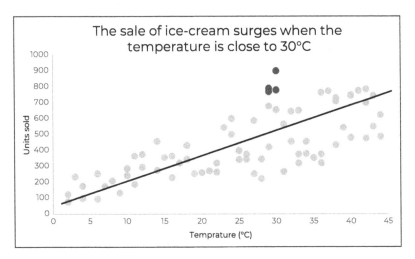

Figure 6.21: Scatter plot highlighting outliers

The same principle applies to the scatter plot in Figure 6.21. The change in color draws attention to a set of outliers, an important part of the story that the data is telling but may otherwise not have been obvious.

Pre-attentive attributes can also be used effectively in bar and column charts to draw your audience's attention to a particular category that you want to hero in your data story (Figure 6.22).

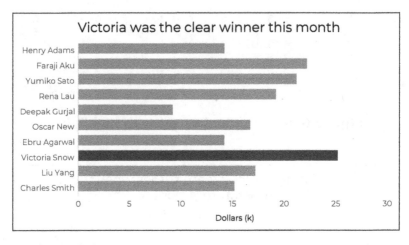

Figure 6.22: Bar chart with highlighted category

Although powerful, these attributes should not be overused as this has the opposite effect. Consider a five-line paragraph of text in a document where half the text is bold and another quarter is underlined. It just becomes confusing. If you highlight everything, nothing becomes important!

Think about the data-ink ratio on a chart

A good chart is clean and easy to read with minimal distraction. Every element on the chart could be considered as "ink." The larger the share of a chart's ink that is devoted to data, the "data ink," the better. Other elements should be considered less important and therefore distracting. The balance of these can be measured using the data-ink ratio.[1]

$$\frac{Data\ ink}{Total\ ink} = Data - ink\ ratio$$

Consider the chart illustrated in Figure 6.23.

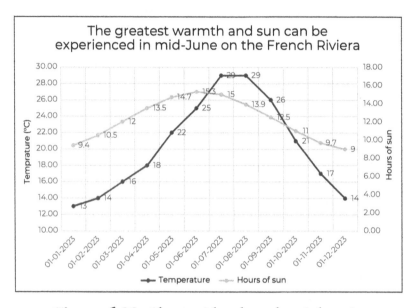

Figure 6.23: Chart with a low data-ink ratio

To maximize the data- ink ratio, eliminate as much irrelevant information as possible, illustrated in Figure 6.24.

- Remove the grid lines.
- Remove unnecessary decimal place on the y-axis.
- Simplify the date format on the x-axis.
- Remove the data labels.

The result: a chart that is much cleaner and easier to read, emphasizing the data that is most important.

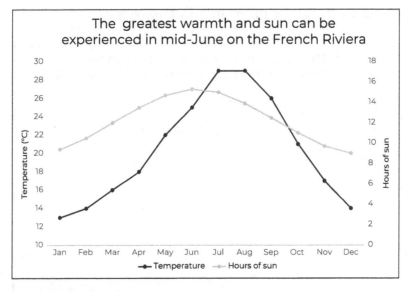

Figures 6.24: Chart with improved data-ink ratio

Other considerations when visualizing data

Other important considerations when preparing charts relate to titles, the use of legends and labels, three-dimensional representations, color combinations, and the poor practice of communicating data in busy matrices.

Charts need strong titles

As we discussed earlier, strong titles play an important role in storytelling. A chart entitled "Monthly sales" is not communicating a message, whereas the title "Monthly sales have increased beyond expectations" is much more meaningful. Make sure that your chart title echoes the most important message being communicated. What would the reader take away by reading the title, alone?

Use a legend, or use labels?

One of the most important measures of effective data visualization is *time-to-insight*, the amount of time that it takes the reader to gain insights from the chart. Clearly, the shorter the time-to-insight, the better.

With this in mind, the use of legends is not recommended (Figure 6.25). When reading the chart, your eyes are forced to jump up and down a few times to identify which line corresponds to which region before you can decode the chart.

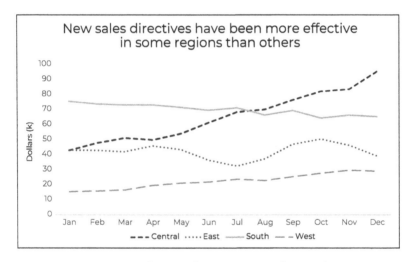

Figure 6.25: Chart using a legend

If we place labels on the trend lines instead, as shown in Figure 6.26, it is much faster to interpret the chart and the time-to-insight is reduced.

The exception to this guideline is a chart has many lines that are close together and there is no space for labels. This is where a legend can be put to good use.

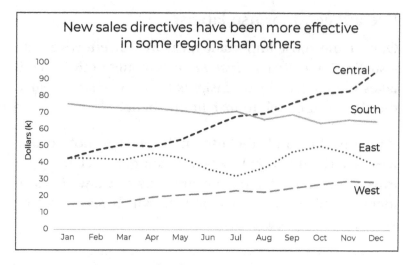

Figure 6.26: Chart using labels

Two dimensions usually work better than three

The eye reads two-dimensional representations much faster than three-dimensional ones. While many graphing applications offer formats such as 3D column and pie charts, these should be avoided. Introducing the third dimension slows down comprehension without introducing any new information in these formats. Only include a third dimension if it brings new information to the chart.

Avoid red and green colors on the same chart

Approximately 8% of men and 0.5% of women are at least partially color-blind.[2] Red-green color blindness is the most prevalent. These people see red and green as a dull brown and are unable to distinguish between the two colors. Avoiding the use of these colors together makes your charts accessible to a wider population.

Busy matrices quickly overload the working memory

Matrices of numbers are useful in situations where it is important to be able to look up an exact value, such as in a spreadsheet or database, however, they are not good for communication purposes. Try to avoid the use of these in documents and presentations.

If you are presenting a matrix containing 25 numbers, but only four of them are relevant to your story, select a better format, such as big numbers. If you want to emphasize a trend, use a line chart. If you're talking about comparison, consider columns or bars.

Chapter summary

The effective visualization of data can play an important role in storytelling.

- Data visualization aims to communicate a message using data. Most data sets contain several different messages. Begin by identifying the message that you want to communicate.

- The visualization system hinges on three types of memory: the iconic memory, the working memory, and the long-term memory.

- Effective visualization aims to appeal to the iconic memory so that it notices what is most important, avoids overloading the working memory, and is therefore successful in reaching the long-term memory.

- There is a wide variety of chart formats available, each suited to a different type of message. Select the correct type of chart for the message that you want to communicate. Make understanding the message as effortless for the reader as possible.

- Pre-attentive attributes can be used to draw attention to the elements most important in the story, creating a hierarchy of visual information.

- The data-ink ratio on a chart compares the data illustrated in the chart with other less relevant or distracting information and should be as high as possible.

- Use strong titles, labels instead of legends where possible, favor 2D representations over 3D, and avoid the use of red and green colors together.

Next steps

Next time you feature data in a story, consider:

- The message that the data should deliver. Don't expect the audience to work it out for themselves.

- The best type of chart to use to convey your message.

- Use of pre-attentive attributes to create a hierarchy of visual information.

Notes

1. E.R. Tufte, *The Visual Display of Quantitative Information* (2nd ed.) (Cheshire, CT: Graphics Press, 2001).
2. Covisn, The color blindness experts, August 11, 2022, www.covisn.com

7 DELIVERING
THE STORY

*Delivering a story requires a degree
of showmanship and the ability to
deal with the unexpected*

CHAPTER SEVEN

DELIVERING THE STORY

Having designed the framework of your story, created support material, crafted a compelling narrative, and considered interaction and navigation approaches, your final task is to execute a successful delivery.

This chapter begins by exploring some practical, yet essential skills required in delivery. It examines the importance of leading your audience, the use of vocal modulation techniques, stage management, the art of smooth question handling, the role of rehearsals, and the ability to work on-camera and deliver stories in virtual settings.

We will return to our case study and observe Jensen's experience when delivering their final presentation to SmartStream.

Finally, four challenging situations are introduced, which are commonly faced during the delivery of stories, with practical strategies for handling them.

Essential skills for a successful delivery

The mechanics of effective presentation

There is a set of basic mechanics that should be mastered to maximize your impact as a storyteller. Some of the most important relate to:

- Leadership
- The ability to convey confidence and enthusiasm
- Managing your audience
- Nervousness and physiological factors

Leadership is essential to impact

The demonstration of leadership is perhaps the most underestimated skill in the delivery of the stories that we tell in business. If you want your audience to listen, be inspired, and be guided by you, your skills as a leader will be essential.

You'll need to adopt the right attitude and get yourself into the right head-space. Find passion in your topic, as passion is contagious. You can't inspire other people unless you are inspired yourself.

If you are speaking on one of your favorite topics, this will probably come naturally. In other cases, you might need to "manufacture" that motivation yourself. Give yourself a pep-talk, if needed. You need to want to be there to deliver the story!

> Some years ago, I was asked to deliver a presentation on operational processes at a seminar in Kuala Lumpur, Malaysia. It was probably the driest topic on the agenda, and the first item after lunch. Hardly a time when the audience was likely to feel energetic! As I walked into the auditorium, I thought to myself *"OK, let's go and talk about processes! It's an important topic and I have some interesting examples to share."* The session was a success, the audience was inspired by my enthusiasm and asked some very interesting questions.

Passion earns the favor of your audience. If you are passionate, you will be liked and even forgiven for any small lapses or mistakes that you make when presenting.

Convey confidence on stage, from the entry to the exit

A good storyteller commands the attention of their audience and conveys confidence on stage. This is achieved through a number of factors such as posture, facial expression, body language, the tone of your voice, and the way that you make eye contact.

Dress code also plays an important role. Are you dressed in a way that is consistent with your role and the expectations of your audience? Are you connecting with them, or surprising them and creating a barrier?

When it's time for you to enter the stage, do so with good posture, smile and walk calmly to your starting point. Make eye contact with your audience and pause for a second to create anticipation before launching into your opening words.

> **Before you even speak, be someone that the audience wants to listen to.**

When it's time for you to leave the stage, pause and acknowledge your audience. If they applaud, smile and give them a moment to express their feelings before you walk away. This is an important moment of recognition for you as a speaker. You deserve it!

Manage your audience: work the room

Leading a session requires you to manage the dialogue with your audience as well as the dialogue between others in the room. If the interaction isn't flowing as it should, it's your job to do something about it. Don't just stand there and watch the boat sink!

If an audience is too quiet, disengaged, or sleepy, start to engage them more. On the other hand, if they are too verbose, disrupting the flow of the session, then you may need to moderate. And if a conflict of opinion occurs between attendees, you're the one who will need to step in and facilitate.

Feeling nervous is natural, but manageable

From time to time all presenters face a situation when they feel nervous. You could be delivering your first presentation, telling a business-critical story to a team of senior executives, or addressing 800 people on a big stage. A little nervousness doesn't have to be a bad thing as it sharpens your focus and performance. Feeling too comfortable or complacent has the opposite effect.

Nervousness is a natural emotion that is almost always short-lived. Once you get going, after a few minutes, you'll find your comfort zone and the nerves will disappear.

Nervous tension usually has the greatest effect on the chest muscles. Your chest tightens up, you feel less comfortable and breathe with less ease. There is a simple exercise that can help to overcome this:

1. About a minute before you begin to present, take a deep breath, filling your lungs with air.

2. Hold it for a second or two.

3. Release it slowly (over several seconds).

4. Repeat the above steps two more times.

The exercise is effective in releasing the tension in your chest and provides instant results. You'll feel better, act more naturally, and be better positioned to deliver your story.

If you find yourself speaking too fast, recover by pausing for a second, taking a breath, and then continuing at a slower pace. Your audience will just think that you are taking a moment to collect your thoughts.

Alternatively, try inserting some form of unplanned interaction to create a dialogue. Ask the audience a question about your topic. A short two-way conversation is a good recovery technique as it breaks the unfamiliar pressure associated with monologue.

Remember that confidence must be built. The best way to build it is to practice and to push yourself out of your comfort zone. Actively seek situations where you will be required to present or consider joining a presentation club. The relief that you feel each time that you succeed will give you the energy needed to push yourself to the next challenge.

Physiological factors should not be underestimated

Presenting with impact requires energy. It requires you to increase your concentration level, to project your voice, and to use your body as you move on stage or camera. Physiological factors therefore require some consideration.

> **Don't make the classic mistake of skipping breakfast, just because you have an important presentation that day.**

For most people this will result in your blood sugar level being too low for you to perform at your best. You don't need to indulge in a feast, but a small snack containing slow-burning carbohydrates (such as fresh fruits) should be enough to give you what you need. Any special medical conditions must, of course, be considered.

Think about your intake of caffeine. Have your morning cup of coffee, but don't have five cups! Elevated levels of caffeine may prevent you from performing calmly and smoothly.

Physical exercise, such as a morning run or a gym workout, can also be helpful a few hours before your session. This helps to get the blood flowing in your brain, warms up your muscles, and releases endorphin which will boost your confidence and the positivity of your mood.

Vocal modulation is an essential skill

The application of a good vocal modulation technique is essential to an accomplished speaker. Make yourself a speaker that others enjoy listening to. Every speaker has their own vocal personality which is created through a combination of attributes.

Speed

Pace your delivery in a way that is thoughtful and unrushed. You know your material, but your audience is hearing it for the first time. They need to be able to hear it and metabolize it. We've all listened to a speaker who raised an interesting point, but we never had the opportunity to reflect on it because they moved on too quickly. Reflection is an important step in the comprehension process and results in improved recollection.

Temporary variations in speed can also be effective, an increase creating the feeling of tension, and a decrease to create emphasis or curiosity around a particular statement.

Volume

Speak with good volume to assert your key ideas. How loudly do you need to project your voice to be heard clearly by your entire audience? Consider the size and layout of the venue. Variations in volume can also be used to communicate emphasis or suspense.

Tonal variation

Tonal variation makes your message more engaging and is essential when conveying emotions such as surprise, anger, or concern. Use the full range of your voice, in particular when citing a dialogue.

Articulation

Use your lips to formulate the words clearly and to avoid mumbling. Professional speakers often perform articulation exercises before stepping onto the stage to warm up the muscles in their lips. When presenting to an audience in their non-native language, this attribute is particularly important.

Pauses

The use of pauses is a powerful vocal modulation technique. Pauses can be used to indicate transition, create emphasis or suspense.

- *Transitional pauses* of 2–3 seconds signal that you have finished covering one point and that you are moving on to the next. This helps the audience organize in their minds the information that you are sharing.

- *Pauses inserted between the words in a phrase* can be used to create emphasis, temporarily slowing down the pace of narration:

People are not signing up to the seminar. I – just – don't – believe it!

- *Theatrical pauses* can be inserted before revealing information to create suspense.

Her family gathered around in anticipation as she opened the envelope and started to read. —"I've been accepted by Harvard!," she gasped.

Training your vocal modulation

Mastering the use of vocal modulation techniques requires some training that will help you to leverage the personality of your voice.

Start by observing performances by professional speakers and their use of these techniques. Tim Urban is an excellent example in his popular TED Talk, "Inside the mind of a master procrastinator."[1] His vocal modulation style makes exceptional use of tonal variation and the timely use of pauses. He also utilizes emotional triggers, largely based on endorphin, dopamine, and adrenalin, and a range of his own personal examples to engage, to inform, and to entertain.

Then train your own vocal modulation using the simple exercise below:

1. Select a narrative that you can present, naturally, from memory lasting no longer than 30–40 seconds. Don't read from notes. You might select the opening words of a presentation that you plan to deliver or the narration of an important point.

2. Record yourself presenting it. Most smartphones contain a voice recorder that is ideal for the task. Adopt the same tone, style, and pace that you would typically use when presenting.

3. Play the recording back and analyze it relative to the parameters discussed above: speed, volume, tonal variation, articulation, and the use of pauses. Don't be put off if you don't like what you hear!

4. Identify one parameter that you think can be improved. Record the same narrative again, focusing on that change.

5. Repeat the exercises five or six times until you are satisfied with end result.

6. Finally, compare your last recording with the first one and observe the difference. Be Inspired by the improvements that you have made.

Consider the importance of non-verbal communication: Stage management, movement, body language and eye contact.

Know how to navigate the stage

If you are presenting on-stage or in a large meeting room, your choice of position will affect the impact that you make on your audience.

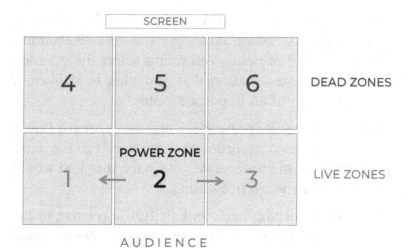

Figure 7.1: The six stage zones

Figure 7.1 provides a bird's-eye view of a typical stage area. Looking down from above, an elevated screen is depicted at the back of the stage where you might display presentation slides. In front of you is the audience. The stage area is divided into six zones.

The three frontal zones, zones 1–3, are the *live* zones. These are the main zones used when presenting. Zone 2 is referred to as the *power zone*, the place from where you can make the best contact with your entire audience.

Always begin and end your presentation from the power zone.

As you speak, move comfortably between the live zones, 1, 2, and 3. Movement should be relaxed and unrushed. This conveys a sense of confidence, at the same time enabling you to engage different sections of the audience.

Avoid zones 4–6, the *dead zones*. The additional distance between these zones and the audience significantly reduces the level of presence that you convey. Only use them if you need to walk to the screen and point something out. Then return to one of the live zones and continue to present from there.

Some speaking venues may have a lectern at the center of the stage. Unless special circumstances warrant it, ask the hosts to remove it. These objects disconnect the speaker from the audience, blocking half of their body language. They also create an overly formal atmosphere and encourage people to read from notes. If the lectern can't be removed, try to stand in front of it.

Smaller venues, such as a meeting room with 10 seats, typically have a smaller stage area utilizing only zones 1–3 and a smaller wall-mounted screen. While you will still open and close from zone 2, zones 1 and 3 will be used predominantly, enabling you to engage the audience without obstructing view of the material presented on-screen.

Body language is an essential part of your communication

An audience not only listens to your words. Your attitude, posture, movement, and the use of gestures to communicate your feelings also form part of your message.

Social psychologist Amy Cuddy emphasizes the importance of body language in her TED Talk, "Your body language may shape who you are."[2]

We are interested in other people's body language.
You need to create a presence. Body language is a
language. Ask yourself: What is your body commu-
nicating to others?

As an experiment, try muting the sound on your television and watching an interview or presentation clip silently. How do you perceive the non-verbal interactions of the people involved?

As you work the stage, the slight exaggeration of certain gestures can help to emphasize important points. For example, shrugging your shoulders when asking a question, raising your arms to convey the feeling of despair or placing your hands in a prayer-like position when appealing to your audience to take an action.

Repetitive gestures such a fidgeting or playing with a pen become distracting and should be avoided. The "fig leaf" position looks awkward. Don't put your hands in your pockets as this restricts your natural arm movements. Would you deliver a presentation wearing handcuffs?

You are always communicating something with your face

It has been said that "the face is the mirror of the soul." We are always communicating something with our faces. We talked earlier about the importance of getting into the right head-space before delivering a story. If you have the right attitude, your face will communicate it.

Avoid smiling too much as this can seem contrived. Smiling a little, as you would passing someone in a corridor, seems human and approachable.

If you are being interviewed, think about your facial expression when you are being asked a question. A slight smile to show interest is the default. Other expressions, depending on the question, whether surprise or amusement, will come naturally.

Eye contact is an essential engagement mechanism

Eye contact is very powerful. You are not engaging with your audience if you don't make eye contact with them. Think of your reaction when someone speaks to you without making eye contact. You naturally feel less inclined to listen.

When presenting to smaller audiences, make eye contact with each individual from time to time. Saying one or two sentences to a person only takes 8–10 seconds and creates direct communication, increasing their engagement.

The technique also works with larger audiences. Look toward different areas of the audience and talk to them in turn. You'll be engaging with a group of people rather than an individual, but you will still be increasing engagement.

Read the room. React to people's smiles, nods, gestures, and in doing so create two-way communication. Increase your focus on people who seem less interested or disengaged. If you don't, they will drift away.

Beware of reading from presentation slides. Glance at your slides when needed, but most of the time you should be making eye contact with the people that you are talking to.

Smooth question handling commands a high degree of credibility

Questions are a natural part of the dialogue with your audience. Don't be put off by them. Questions can be highly relevant and add to the exploration of your topic but can also be difficult or disruptive. We will explore four of the more challenging situations later in the chapter, but first let's discuss some basic question handling techniques.

When a presenter is asked a question, remember that she has a choice . . .

The five most common responses are:

1. **Answer the question:** When the question is relevant to the discussion at hand and can be answered without consuming excessive time.

2. **Defer it professionally:** When the question will be answered in a later part of the story and is better handled then. Be sure to defer it professionally.

   That's a good question. In a few minutes time we'll be dealing with that topic in detail. May I come back to your question at that point?

3. **Take it offline:** When the question is relevant, but extremely specific. It would take a long time to answer, and the answer would not be of interest to most of the people in your audience.

That's a good question. As it's quite detailed, could we talk offline at the end of the session? I'd be happy to discuss it.

4. **Take an action item:** If you don't know the answer you may need to take an action item, do some research, and provide an answer at a later time.

5. **Throw the question back to the audience:** When you have a knowledgeable audience, you can put them to work and start a dialogue. This technique works well if you don't know the answer to a question, but you are pretty sure that someone in the audience will.

That's an interesting question. Does anyone in the room have a position on that?

These approaches provide a basic, yet systematic mechanism for question handling. It's like playing tennis. Every time the ball approaches you, you make a conscious decision on which way to deflect it. Questions handling works in much the same way.

Rehearsals can play an important role

If you are delivering a story on a topic that you know well or have delivered many times before, you are probably well prepared to just stand up and speak. But for a critical presentation or keynote that you are delivering for the first time, rehearsals can play an important role.

Know the key points that you plan to cover, but don't memorize your narrative word by word. The brain memorizes ideas better than prose. As a dynamic speaker, you will most likely use slightly different words each time you deliver the story. What's most important is that you get you key points across.

Record your talk using both audio and video if possible and analyze your performance. Prepare until you feel comfortable that you could more or less deliver it in your sleep! Most TED Talks are rehearsed 20–30 times before they ever reach the stage. This is no accident, but an important quality measure required by the organizers.

Virtual settings require a degree of adaptation

In a hybrid world comprising both face-to-face and virtual settings, many meetings and presentations are conducted using virtual media. Some additional considerations are required when working in these environments.

Camera on or off?

Virtual meetings aim to use today's technology to simulate an in-person experience as closely as possible. Don't shy away from using your camera. As a presenter, always have your camera switched on.

During longer meetings when you are listening, not speaking, you may prefer to switch your camera off, but always switch it on again when speaking or asking a question.

Frame yourself on camera

An important aspect of working the camera is to frame yourself correctly.

The height of your camera, whether built-in to a laptop or external, should be at nose level. This enables you to make eye contact straight into the camera. For those using a laptop camera this usually means elevating your computer by 3-4 inches from the surface of your desk. A small platform can be used, or even a stack of books will serve the purpose.

When angling the camera, make sure that you don't have too much vertical space over your head. Allow just enough space to make sure that the top of your head isn't clipped. Your head, shoulders, and upper arms should be visible. Adjust your distance from the camera if necessary.

Sit with your elbows slightly wider apart than usual, increasing your physical size. This is referred to as *dominating the frame* and communicates confidence (Figure 7.2).

Figure 7.2: Framing on camera

Move your head naturally when you speak to avoid looking static and be aware that you may need to lift your hands a little higher than usual when making gestures to capture them in the frame.

You probably have a comfortable chair at your desk but avoid swiveling or reclining as you speak. This is distracting and de-frames you. Keep an upright position with good posture.

Actively control the lighting situation

Make sure that you have the right amount of light on your face. If you are facing a window on a sunny day, this won't be a problem, but for other situations you may need to invest in a studio light, many of which look like a glowing doughnut on a stick. These are inexpensive and allow you to adjust both the brightness and the color temperature of the light.

Make good eye contact with the camera

You should be looking directly into the camera at least 70% of the time. You are talking to your audience. You may need to glance away from time to time to refer to your notes or look at another screen but keep this brief. Avoid looking downward or to the side for extended periods of time.

Case study: Jensen's presentation to SmartStream

The Jensen team has everything in place for the delivery of their story. At the same time, the world of business is unpredictable. You never know exactly what's going to be on the minds of your audience when you step forward to deliver. Priorities may have shifted and resistance to new ideas or even political agendas may be encountered.

> **It's good preparation, plus the ability to navigate around obstacles during the delivery of a story that lead to a successful outcome.**

Recommendation first or last?

As discussed in Chapter 4, the delivery of a story brings with it a choice: to begin with the recommendation or to end with it?

Jensen knows that some of SmartStream's executives strongly favor the move to buy a new billing system and therefore chooses the second approach.

Check points are important during the delivery

Taking regular check points is an important when delivering a story. It's the mechanism that keeps the audience in synch with the presenter.

Jensen plans to take a check point after each step in the deductive flow of their story which will also make the delivery easier. A two-way dialogue is more natural than a monologue. This will also provide a more immediate opportunity to address any questions or concerns that arise along the way.

Anticipation of likely questions and any required support material

If you are delivering your story in presentation format, "hidden" slides may sometimes be included with the additional detail required to answer these questions well. These slides will only be presented if the related questions arise but demonstrate a robust and well-prepared approach.

Jensen has prepared two such slides: One containing in-depth analysis concerning the unsuitability of a new system. A second explaining additional details of the proposed upgrade path.

Delivering the final presentation to SmartStream

The Jensen team arrives at SmartStream's headquarters office to deliver their final presentation. Peter Lewin, leading the project, is accompanied by two colleagues, Rebecca Huang and Timur Saad, both senior analysts who have contributed to the work presented. Eight executives from SmartStream will participate, including Kristian Sorenson (CEO), Kristina Lassen (CMO), and Nils Mortensson (CIO).

They organize their delivery using the five presentation phases introduced in Chapter 5. Peter takes the lead.

Opening words

His opening address is:

"SmartStream aims to secure its leading position through the introduction of enhanced billing

capabilities. We see this as a critical and timely move given current market conditions."

Peter has selected these words to set the tone of the session and also to create a sense of urgency around the topic.

Presenter introductions

He then proceeds to introduce himself and his team:

"My name is Peter Lewin. I'm leading the team at Jensen Consulting responsible for this important assignment. I bring 15 years of experience from the technology industry, specifically in the billing area."

"With me today are Rebecca Huang and Timur Saad, both senior analysts who have contributed to this assignment. Rebecca has nine years of experience and has just returned from an assignment in Beijing where she helped a client define a complete set of billing process for a cable-TV operator."

"Timur brings eight years of experience in marketing and content management. He has taken the lead in exploring the new services that you will need to offer to your customers to remain competitive and the billing capabilities that will be required to deliver them."

The credentials of the team have been established through introductions that are objective, tangible, relevant, and concise.

Topic introduction

Peter now introduces the topic:

> *"The solution that we are going to propose to you today will enable you to meet your short- and medium-term needs in the billing area. You have communicated these needs very clearly in our earlier discussions with your marketing, operations, and technology organizations. We'll be showing you how we have used that input together with our industry experience to define the best approach for SmartStream."*

The topic introduction has been crafted to connect with the needs of the receiving audience, and to secure their full attention.

Main body

The main body of the presentation follows the flow of the story blueprint created earlier.

Timur takes the stage and begins to talk about Smart-Stream's business drivers for the initiative, utilizing both their audience understanding (captured in step 2 of the methodology), and co-creation activities (captured in step 3).

> *"We have based our analysis on your business priorities. Improved customer centricity and faster time to market have been emphasized by those of you in marketing, as well as the need to offer more flexible billing formats and customized tariffs. Scalability has been a concern voiced by your technology organization as you grow and enter new markets."*

He then takes a check point with his audience:

"Would you agree that these are your main priorities?"

The executives nod in agreement. Their CEO, Kristian, makes a comment:

"I think that you have understood our business direction very well. Something that I would like to emphasize is that cost reduction will be particularly important. We aim to expand our business with a focus on profitable growth."

Timur acknowledges the feedback while one of his colleagues makes a note. The feedback obtained will enable them to build additional flexibility into their delivery. As the story unfolds, they will place additional emphasis on items related to cost reduction. He continues:

"Based on your business priorities, we have identified the system functionalities that you will need to implement as well as the additional capacity that you are likely to need."

"The proposed on-line portal will be important. It will enable you to develop closer relationships with your customers, to up-sell and cross-sell, without putting additional load on your call centers."

"Customized tariffs and flexible billing formats such as electronic and consolidated bills will be essential in dominating the B2B (business-to-business)

segment. Free trials will enable you to attract new customers, giving them the chance to experience new services and content. And our estimates suggest a need to support up to six million subscribers within the next three years."

The audience signals agreement. In this case, no formal check point is needed. Peter now takes over, responsible for the next part of the delivery:

"As you are aware, two deployment approaches have been identified: either to replace your existing billing system, or to upgrade the system that you have today."

"The findings of our analysis suggest that a new system is unfeasible at this time due to a high associated cost, lengthy implementation time, extensive training required for your staff, and the complex migration of data from the old system to a new one."

At this point, Nils, SmartStream's CIO, raises an objection:

"I'm not sure that I agree. Would a new system really be unaffordable? Our current system is aging and will have to be replaced sooner or later. There are replacement systems on the market today that would fulfill our needs. Is it wise to invest further in the maintenance of old technology?"

The Jensen team had anticipated this potential objection. Displaying one of their hidden slides, Peter narrates the information displayed on-screen:

"The left of this figure shows a detailed financial comparison between the two options. A new system is the more expensive option, but as you say, this is not necessarily unfeasible for SmartStream."

"But take a look at the implementation analysis on the right. The real concern is time. Implementing a new system would take an estimated 16 months. Your competitors are gaining ground quickly and would likely overtake you in some of your markets by then. Swift action is needed. By performing an upgrade quickly, and bringing urgently needed capabilities to market, you would be able to secure your position and then plan for a full replacement in 2–3 years."

The executives are satisfied with this answer, backed up by hard evidence. The concern has been addressed.

Rebecca delivers the final part of the story summarizing the additional benefits associated with the upgrade and outlines a project implementation plan.

The summary: closing words

Peter delivers a summary that brings a new angle to what has been discussed and adds a clear and specific call-to-action:

"The recommendation presented today can be a powerful move in advancing SmartStream's market position, if executed quickly. Take this recommendation back to your respective teams and discuss it in detail. Focus on the activities that you consider most crucial, estimate the resources that you will need to

commit to this initiative and identify any risks or obstacles that you foresee. Bring this input to our next meeting on 1st March where we can begin the development of an implementation plan."

Final questions are addressed and Peter thanks the executives for participating, on behalf of his team. Smart-Stream is satisfied with the outcome and Jensen's initial task has been completed.

Challenging situations when delivering a story

The Jensen team faced a relatively smooth delivery experience, but this may not always be the case.

> **Even in the light of good preparation, the delivery of a story will not always be "a walk in the park."**

Four short case examples below discuss common challenges and strategies for dealing with them:

- Continuous interruptions from the audience
- Responding to strong disagreement
- A conflict between two audience participants
- Hostile objections and political agendas.

Continuous interruptions from the audience

Nick, a restaurant manager at a leading hotel resort in South Africa, is presenting some upcoming changes to operational procedures to his team of 20 staff. He has only one hour, and a lot of information to share.

Each topic in his presentation attracts numerous questions from the team, concerned about the impact on their daily roles. The audience is taking over. Addressing all of their questions would prevent him from delivering this important briefing.

As we have discussed, managing your audience is an important leadership task when you deliver a story. An anxious audience could easily overwhelm you with questions and prevent you from delivering your content.

Many suggest that in a situation like this the presenter should close the floor saying, *"Please hold all questions to the end of the session."* While this might be convenient for the presenter, allowing them to present without interruption, it may also de-rail your ability to achieve the vision of your story.

By silencing your audience, you destroy the two-way dialogue needed to secure their interest and commitment.

If you expect your audience to sit and listen silently for 30 minutes, you will probably lose them, at least for some of the time. Long monologues are uninteresting. People's minds wander and they lose focus. A better approach is to insert short, intermittent, Q&A (question and answer) windows into your delivery.

"You have a lot of good questions, which is great," Nick responds. "But I also have a lot of important information to share with you today. Could I ask that you hold your questions, and every 10 minutes we will insert a short Q&A session to pick some of them up?"

When you run your first Q&A session and invite questions, ten hands might shoot up, but perhaps you decide only to take the first three questions. *"Given the limited time, we now need to move on,"* you explain.

This approach balances the need to present your content with the equally important need to maintain a dialogue that engages your audience.

Reacting to strong disagreement

Chantal, a marketing specialist, is presenting a social media strategy to the management team of a pharmaceutical company in Belgium. She begins her presentation but the head of media, Marc Wouters, quickly voices strong disagreement.

"I saw this approach applied in a project last year," he says. *"It was a complete failure. This will never work!"*

Chantal tries to address his concern, but his position remains firm and unchanged. *"This would be disastrous,"* he maintains. The rest of the audience waits in anticipation to see how she will react.

Strong opinions may surround the topics that we present in stories. Sometimes concerns can be addressed straightaway, but in other cases not. At the same time, it is important to ensure that critique does not damage the credibility of the presenter in the eyes of the wider audience.

> You won't be able to reach agreement with everyone in your session on every topic. The ability to "agree to disagree" therefore becomes important.

It is important to acknowledge an opposing opinion before putting forward your own view. Avoid a defensive attitude, even if it is your first instinct. Otherwise the dialogue can easily escalate into an unnecessary conflict.

> *"Thank you for sharing that experience, which is very interesting,"* Chantal responds. *"Over the last few years we have seen this approach work very well in a number of our projects,"* she explains. *"But if you have concerns or would like to see some examples of the work, I would be pleased to provide them offline."*

Marc, although still not in agreement, parks his objection. The wider audience is impressed by Chantal's professionalism and willingness to address his concern.

A conflict between two audience participants

> A team of auditors was hired to review the progress of a large, strategic project in Latin America. The project was facing challenges that threatened its profitability. Management was seeking an external view and recommendations on the best recovery strategy and to get the project back on track.
>
> After completing four weeks of analysis, the audit team arrived at the boardroom to present their

findings to seven senior executives. It wasn't going to be an easy story to present. A classic example of a "bad news presentation." The project concerned had been poorly managed and their findings were far from promising.

Hugo, the lead auditor, began the presentation, displaying a dashboard of audit scores and status indicators, many of which were red.

The VP (Vice President) of Sales, a large and intimidating-looking man, reacted immediately. He began shouting with a booming voice, but not at Hugo. Instead pointing across the table to his counterpart, the VP of Service Delivery.

"This is brilliant," he gasped. *"Finally, the truth is on the table! If your people would do their jobs, we wouldn't have to look at figures like this!"*

The VP of Service Delivery attempted, with good reason, to defend her organization. Her team was certainly not the sole reason for the issue. But the VP of Sales became more agitated by her defence. As the conflict escalated with more shouting and accusations, the VP of Service Delivery broke down in tears of frustration.

An uncomfortable situation for Hugo and his team. Unless handled carefully the conflict could take over the session and prevent the delivery from being fully completed. It's usually wise to wait a moment or two before intervening in these situations. Many naturally subside. If not, you may need to take action.

As a leader, if your session is not progressing in a constructive direction, it's your job to step in.

After a few moments Hugo interjected. *"Please . . .,"* he said. *"I recognize that you have different opinions, but we are not here to point fingers. We are here to find solutions. Bear with us for just a few minutes. Let us walk you through the rest of the results, some of which are very positive. Then we can put our heads together and discuss the best way forward."*

Having been reminded that their common purpose, and the reason for the audit, was to get an important project back on track, the two executives agreed to put aside their differences, albeit with some hesitation, and allow the presentation to continue.

Hostile objections and political agendas

A human resources (HR) team at a large cosmetics company in Sweden was proposing a new initiative to a group of departmental heads in their organization.

The initiative aimed to reduce the high rate of employee churn and loss of talent, but required several policy changes related to compensation, career advancement opportunities, recognition, and the delegation of responsibility.

Of the six heads, one was particularly resentful of the initiative. She felt that it would cause unnecessary turbulence and disrupt the status quo in her department.

As Ludwig, the leader of the HR team, proceeded through the delivery, she continually attacked the ideas presented. When a project timeline was proposed, her immediate response was, *"You will never achieve this."* When a new career advancement model was described, she said, *"My people will not accept this."* And when changes to compensation were introduced, she just laughed out loud.

Her open hostility toward the initiative created an awkward atmosphere in the room and a difficult situation for Ludwig and his co-workers.

Encountering resistance when delivering a story is not uncommon. In some cases, one or more participants may attend your session purely with the intention of being disruptive. Handle these situations carefully, particularly if the individuals concerned hold high rank within your audience. Don't be tempted to fight fire with fire!

Ludwig maintained a positive and calm approach as these reactions were received. He listened and acknowledged her opinions, asking questions to fully understand her position when needed. Concerns that could be addressed were addressed with solid responses, based on good preparation. Unexpected concerns that needed further investigation were taken offline as action items.

The ability to address concerns smoothly is an important skill when delivering a story.

Interestingly, the approach was effective in winning additional support from the other departmental heads. They could see that change was needed and realized that their colleague was just being difficult. The good answers provided, together with a constructive reaction to criticism, created confidence in the recommendations being presented.

Chapter summary

Excellence in the delivery of a story requires a combination of good showmanship and flexibility. To achieve this, follow these steps.

Master a robust set of presentation mechanics

- Adopt a mindset that allows you to convey both leadership and confidence. To inspire others, you need to be inspired yourself.

- Master vocal modulation techniques to leverage the personality of your voice. Think about speed, volume, tonal variation, articulation, and the use of pauses.

- Use the different zones on the stage to maximize your impact. Work from the live zones, avoid the dead zones.

- Apply good practices related to the eye contact that you make with your audience, movement, and body language.

- Adopt a systematic approach to the handling of questions: Answer, defer, take an offline discussion or an action item, throw to the audience, or politely decline with an explanation if the question is outside your scope.

- Frame yourself well on camera when working in virtual settings. Get into the habit of dominating the frame. This will increase your impact significantly.

When delivering the story, take your audience on a journey

- Decide when check points are needed to keep your audience engaged and in synch with your delivery.

- Try to secure acceptance at each stage. This is much more effective than presenting the whole story and then asking, "Do you agree?" at the end.

- Anticipate likely questions and be ready to answer them. Develop additional "hidden" support material if needed, to address these questions well.

Be aware of common challenges and strategies for handling them

- Continuous interruptions from the audience can be addressed with intermittent question & answer sessions.

- In the face of strong disagreement, you may need to "agree to disagree" so that your delivery can continue.

- If a conflict arises between two audience participants, wait to see if they can resolve it quickly themselves, otherwise leverage your role as the leader of the session and facilitate.

- If you encounter hostile objections or political agendas, handle them calmly and professionally. Always acknowledge and then address concerns where possible.

Next steps

- Integrate the practices discussed in this chapter into your own, personal delivery style.

- Use the exercise provided to record and analyze your own voice to develop your vocal modulation technique.

- If you participate in virtual meetings or deliveries, optimize your broadcast environment and framing approach.

Notes

1. Tim Urban, "Inside the mind of a master procrastinator." TED Talk, 2016. www.youtube.com/watch?v=arj7oStGLkU
2. Amy Cuddy, "Your body language may shape who you are." TED Global, 2012. www.youtube.com/watch?v=Ks-_Mh1QhMc

COMPLETION CHECKLIST

Congratulations! You have just completed *The Ultimate Guide to Storytelling in Business*. This book aimed to equip you with a practical set of storytelling skills using a well-proven methodology based on seven logical steps.

Use the checklist below as a self-assessment. For any items that you are unable to check off, review the guidelines in the corresponding chapter.

Defining the vision

☐ I know how to define an outcome-oriented vision for a story.

Understanding your audience

☐ I know how to profile an audience and identify audience-specific information that can be incorporated to ensure that the story will resonate with my audience.

Framing the problem

☐ I know how to build a logic tree.

☐ I know how to use the tree as part of a co-creation session, marking feedback on the diagram in real time and aligning with the needs and priorities of my audience.

Constructing a story framework

☐ I understand the difference between the deductive and inductive methods and know how to test each type of argument to ensure that it is robust enough to include in a story.

☐ I know how to combine these methods into a one-page story blueprint.

☐ I know how to translate the blueprint into the structure of a report or presentation.

☐ I understand the importance of strong titles when documenting a story.

Preparing an engaging delivery

☐ I understand the importance of opening words in setting the tone for the delivery. I am familiar with the eight most common approaches.

☐ I am aware of the four characteristics of a well-crafted speaker introduction and can apply them to my own personal situation.

☐ I know how to craft a topic introduction that presents a value proposition to my audience, giving them a good reason to listen.

☐ I am familiar with the different linguistic structures available for use in the narrative and can apply them to make my story more relatable.

☐ I am familiar with the five principal neurochemicals used in storytelling and can combine them into emotional triggers that will influence the feelings and reactions of my audience.

☐ I understand the role of descriptive detail, personalization, and the use of characters when designing a narrative.

☐ I understand the importance of designing interaction and navigation approaches before the delivery of a story.

Visualizing data

☐ I understand the relationships between the iconic, working, and long-term memories.

☐ I am familiar with the use of some of the most common chart types, and their nuances.

☐ I understand how to use pre-attentive attributes to guide the focus of my audience, ensuring that they understand my intended message quickly.

Delivering the story

☐ I understand the importance of leadership when delivering stories in the business context.

☐ I have mastered a good vocal modulation technique and have completed the "record your own voice" exercise.

☐ I know how to use the different zones of the stage when presenting, and how to maximize my impact when working in virtual situations on camera.

☐ I am familiar with the five most common approaches for handling questions during a presentation.

☐ I am familiar with approaches for dealing with continuous interruptions, strong disagreement, conflicts between participants, and hostile critique.

Of the 23 points listed, how many did you score?

Samir Parikh and his team regularly delivery
high-impact training workshops on the topic
of storytelling for leading corporations. They
also support organizations in the development
of keynote addresses, presentations and other
materials to address lucrative opportunities
within their own areas of specialization.

The workshops, now delivered in more than 50
countries, provide practical skills for immediate
application using a mix of discussions, business
simulations, individual exercises and industry case
studies. Participants also apply their skills to a
personal job-related story that they will need to
deliver with excellence in the near future.

To learn more about developing the
game-changing skill of storytelling within
your organization, consult www
.spconsulting.se/storytelling

INDEX